PENGUIN BOOKS

FORCED ENTRIES

Poet, musician, and diarist Jim Carroll was born and grew up in New York City. Talented at both basketball and writing, he attended Trinity High School in Manhattan on a scholarship and was an All-City basketball star—a period in his life vividly described in his widely praised book *The Basketball Diaries*, which became a national bestseller when a movie version starring Leonardo DiCaprio was released in 1995. Caroll's first collection of poetry, *Living at the Movies*, was published in 1973 when he was twenty-two. His other books include *The Book of Nods* (1986), *Fear of Dreaming: The Selected Poems of Jim Carroll* (1993), and *Void of Course* (1998). His works have appeared in such publications as *Rolling Stone, Poetry*, and *The Paris Review*; in the film *Poetry in Motion*; and on the album *Life Is a Killer*. As leader of the Jim Carroll Band, he recorded three albums for Atlantic Records, *Catholic Boy, Dry Dreams*, and *I Write Your Name. Praying Mantis*, a spoken-word recording, was released by Giant Records in 1991. *A World Without Gravity: The Best of the Jim Carroll Band* was released by Rhino Records in 1993. Mercury Records will release a new recording by Jim Carroll in the fall of 1998.

Books by Jim Carroll

Living at the Movies
The Basketball Diaries
The Book of Nods
Forced Entries: The Downtown Diaries 1971–1973
Fear of Dreaming: The Selected Poems of Jim Carroll

FORCED ENTRIES: THE DOWNTOWN DIARIES 1971-1973

JIM CARROLL

PENGUIN BOOKS

PENGUIN BOOKS
Published by the Penguin Group
Penguin Putnam, Inc.,
375 Hudson Street, New York, New York 10014, U.S.A.
Penguin Books Ltd, 27 Wrights Lane, London W8 5TZ, England
Penguin Books Australia Ltd, Ringwood,
Victoria, Australia
Penguin Books Canada Ltd, 10 Alcorn Avenue,
Toronto, Ontario, Canada M4V 3B2
Penguin Books (N.Z.) Ltd, 182–190 Wairau Road,
Auckland 10, New Zealand
Penguin India, 210 Chiranjiv Tower,
43 Nehru Place, New Delhi 11009, India

Penguin Books Ltd, Registered Offices:
Harmondsworth, Middlesex, England

First published in Penguin Books 1987
Published simultaneously in Canada

20   19   18   17

LIBRARY OF CONGRESS CATALOGING IN PUBLICATION DATA
Carroll, Jim.
  Forced entries.
  I. Title.
PS3553.A7644F6   1987   813'.54   86-30465
ISBN 0 14 00.8502 5

Printed in the United States of America
Set in Baskerville

To Clarice Rivers

AUTHOR'S NOTE

Because I know from repeated experience one question which will be asked later, I will try to answer it now. This diary is not the literal truth and is not meant to be a historical recounting of the period. The entries were consciously embellished and fictionalized to some extent. My purpose was simply to convey the texture of my experiences and feelings for that period.

The events in this book took place, as indicated, from 1971 to 1973. It should be made clear, however, that, within this time frame, the chronological order of the diary entries themselves is not 100 percent accurate. A few may have taken place either before or after their places in the present sequence. On the whole, I think they are in as close to an accurate order as is necessary. That is, it does not make any difference as far as the overall story is concerned.

Although I have a very solid memory for dialogue, I did, at times, have to reconstruct things said, and gave in to some temptations to "go off" a bit, mainly for the sake of humor. Humor, I've found, has an uncanny ability to create its own energy and push on a writer against his will.

Finally, in my previous book of diaries, I fortunately did not have to deal with the matter of public personalities. The point that I would just as soon have preferred not to do so in this book is academic. They were there and so was I. The fact is that I have changed all the names except where that change seemed ludicrous (e.g., Warhol) or where it would rob the reader of an image integral to the piece (e.g., Allen Ginsberg). Many of the characters also are composite figures, both in physical appearance and personal habits. I think it is better this way (for you, the reader): it makes it easier *to make the characters your own.*

I sincerely hope this has not answered all your questions.

The author wishes to thank Rosemary Carroll and Susan Friedland.

A special thanks to Tamela for her dedication, perception and inspiration.

A BIRTHDAY

This is the day I was born, twenty years ago in Bellevue
hospital, New York City, at three minutes past midnight.
It's the birthday of Herman Melville, the Emperor Clau-
dius, and Mr. Jerry Garcia of The Grateful Dead. This is
also the day the Russians scattered the remnants of their
first bomb into the atmosphere. They detonated it, in fact,
only a few hours after I was pulled from my mother's
womb, and the radiation, fear, and the fire's desperate heat
have been there ever since.

I celebrated with a birthday gift from my aunt, twenty
dollars which conveniently arrived in the morning's mail.
I tipped over to Spanish Hector's place to score, and Hector, knowing it was my birthday (since I took the pains to
tell him in both English and Spanish), gave me an extra
five-dollar bag for my money. "It's good stuff," he said,
"from my own stash. I haven't had a chance to put a single
whack on it."

He also offered to throw a few party lines of coke into
the cooker as I was preparing a shot in his kitchen. I passed
on that, however. I have never liked speedballs, the com-
bining of cocaine and heroin in a single shot. I always felt
it was like spreading applesauce all over a good pork chop.
When it comes to heroin, I'm as strict a purist as those
ersatz folkies who booed Dylan off the stage at Newport
for using an electric guitar. I don't like to dilute the essential
rush.

Besides, I've never understood what the rage about co-caine was all about. All it does for me is get my kneecaps high. Coke is just methedrine with a better alibi.

The dope was as good as Hector said. On the way back over to my room at the Chelsea I saw an owl on Seventh Avenue. It was doing a little gymnastic routine on a lamp post.

The fact is, in many ways, I hadn't planned to make it to this age. I think of my past as if it were some exquisite antique knife . . . you can use it to defend yourself or slit your own throat, but you can't just keep it mounted on some wall. I can no longer allow the past, however, to interpret my future. Not dying young can be a dilemma.

Such notions, I see now, are an indulgence. I inhabit a different body now. Each day, it seems, another self wakes up and heats the coffee. I can distinguish, even gauge, the passage from a disturbed youth to a disturbed adult by the subtle aggressiveness in my anxiety. Sometimes I catch my-self sitting on the edge of the sofa, staring into the flickering glare of the television, like a deer on some highway trans-fixed in shock by the headlights of a car. As these images pass, I can feel them feeding my own inertia. Other times, I am overloaded with a smooth, graceful energy, filled with an almost incomprehensible joy.

So, having lived, it seems only proper to begin keeping track again, to record the flux of each self, and weigh the shifting landscape of this city. I've given much of myself to feed its insatiable, tick-ridden underbelly, and I expect the use of its character, without threats or intimidation, in return. If you haven't died by an age thought predeter-mined through the timing of your abuses and excesses, then what else is left but to begin another diary?

JENNY ANN, LIKE A CAT

This morning, in what has become a daily ritual, Jenny Ann came by my room at the Chelsea, bearing my usual breakfast, before she took off for work at the art supply store uptown. She brought with her all my morning staples—two light and sweet coffees, two chocolate donuts (one laced with coconut flakes), and a pint of chocolate Italian ice from the pizza stand across 23rd Street. I drank the coffee, allowing the ice to melt a bit into the desired consistency, and proceeded to stuff down the rest. As I slurped the last of the ice, which I had supplemented with bite-size bits of donut, Jenny Ann laid out twenty-five dollars on the desk.

"This was all I could make, without bringing something down on me, out of the register yesterday. I'll be able to do better today . . . the prick who's over my head there is off."

I told her that the twenty-five would do fine until the evening; there was no way I could tell her how sweet and special I thought she was. All the women always assure me at first how they don't care if I'm using junk, probably thinking they'll be *the one* with the power to transform me back to the wholesome life. And, just as certain, within a week . . . two at the most, they're bitching about how they can't handle it anymore, how the shit is erecting a larger and larger barrier between us, and, speaking of "erecting," how they're not getting laid since I'm on the continual nod half the time, and writing all that crazy bullshit the other half. Besides the hypocrisy involved here, it is all quite inelegant, to say the least. I mean, *they* made the assurances, not I. And to cast such aspersion on my work ("crazy bullshit," indeed), is simply the bitter fruit of sexual frustration revealing itself. An ugly cycle of mounting tensions, which invariably explodes, in time, into a contest of pure hate, where every mask is removed and both people simply lose, having shown more of themselves than anyone should. Resentment . . . sly words . . . lies . . . stomped vulnerabilities . . . violence . . . fine. Ah, but Jenny Ann, none of this for her. She is as clear with her destiny as I with mine. And that destiny is, like her energy (which I sadly lack), unlimited. All that is needed for her is time, and judgment. Meanwhile, we touch each other.

She seems to have accepted fully my advice to concentrate on writing now, putting aside her drawings for the time being. She possesses something else which causes me great envy, it being another quality I am in too short supply of—ambition. The best and healthiest kind of ambition, you must understand. Ambition totally integral to her vision, and the work which is manifestation of that vision. It is a sad thing that I take her money to score a drug she will (I pray) never approach any need for. Sometimes I open my eyes out of a deep nod and see her staring down at me as if, by some vicarious means, by some force built out of an overwhelming will, she herself had penetrated the flux of my drug dreams and shared them in each vivid detail. It is as if I were riding a raft through rapids and, by a supernatural sense of timing and dexterity, she jumped onto it from a bridge as I passed beneath it, having followed it from above a long time before, as it first came into view around a great curve. And she lands feet first, upright, like a cat.

A DAY AT THE RACES

The French call them *papillons d'amour,* i.e., the "butterflies of love." I call them crabs, the tiny parasites of crotch. Jenny Ann noticed them first. Last night she snagged one as it broke loose from the camouflage of her jet black pubic underbrush and slowly tried to patrol the crevice of a scar from a past Caesarian birth, like a scout soldier traversing a trench. She seized it hostage, placing it in a specimen jar, and proceeded through deep infiltration to raid the hirsute main camp . . . at first taking more prisoners, then proceeding to a harsher, yet more expedient, tactic of strict search and destroy. She arrived at my room in the Chelsea this morning with jar in hand.

After a short briefing, she removed from her bag a pocket

flashlight and magnifying glass. I was ordered to remove my pants. The search began immediately, with a great enthusiasm and vigor on her part. My blondish pubes made the job, from a visual standpoint, a snap . . . so to speak. I was skeptical, however, that I could be a carrier of said invaders.

"You're wasting your time; I'm clean," I offered patiently.

"Oh yes, well what's that there?" she replied.

"That's a tiny blackhead is all." I peered closely with the glass.

"It's a moving blackhead, then . . . check it out."

She was right. I was shocked. I felt hygiene-deficient. I wondered who gave what to whom, but no sense looking for blame. We were in this together. It felt sort of sweet, sharing such an affliction. I held still as Jenny Ann removed the visible parties. It hurt a bit. They had burrowed deep into the pores. Apparently, we had been the hosts of a tenacious strain. Finally, she resorted to tweezers, depositing the captives in a separate jar which had a picture of a beaming baby's face on it and was labeled "stewed carrots." I asked her why she was saving the little buggers (which, on close examination, *did,* indeed, bear an uncanny resemblance to the common crab. As far as the French are concerned, I can say in all honesty that not even Nabokov has ever seen a butterfly that looked remotely like these creatures). "You'll see," she answered, "just let me rub in some of this lotion I borrowed from Roger." It was a wonderful manner by which to be medicated. My cock quickly stood erect, which was fortunate . . . we discovered two stragglers hiding beneath the base of it.

With the application done, Jenny Ann removed one of the residents of her jar. "Now you pick one," she looked over, "make sure he's a lively type. We're gonna have a race."

I picked out a trooper who had been circling restlessly around the bottom of the jar. We took a long sheet of

drawing paper from Jenny's portfolio and drew a line down
the center. The first race was the twelve-inch sprint. We
laid down the paper so that our pubic hair awaited at the
finish line, an incentive. My crab ran like a fix, falling off
the edge halfway through the race. Jenny's was in tip-top
form. He came in clocked at twenty-three seconds. We
spent the next hour establishing the best of our stables,
and enjoyed the rest of the day at the races. What a woman,
who can turn an ailment into a viable recreation.

THE CANCER HALL OF FAME

Jenny Ann stood in the kitchenette, pouring the coffee
from its monstrous container into a more manageable cup.
She looked sad, her eyes missing that glowing, stand-up
quality. They were like heliotropes, bent and frayed, shud-
dering under a bank of clouds.

"I'm concerned about Roger . . . really worried, in fact,"
she spoke, a fake distraction in her voice. "He was back up
at *that* place again last night . . . that makes five, no six,
nights in a row, counting the first night with you and I."

"Is he acting weird or something," I asked.

"Not really," Jenny replied, "I mean, he paces a
lot . . . don't sleep much . . ."

"He's always been like *that,*" I threw back, lowering my
voice as she brought the coffee over to the bed. "Nothing
new there."

"Well, he does *sneeze* a lot lately," she countered, "and,
besides, isn't just going up to that dreadful place every
night acting weird enough?"

"That's a point . . . that is definitely a point."

Let me tell you a bit about Roger before I get into this
place that Jenny keeps referring to. He was lovers with her
when they both moved into their loft after dropping out
of the same art school, but then Roger decided he was
completely, irremediably gay, so they began sleeping in separate beds and erected an amicable, thin plaster wall be-

tween their two work spaces. Roger has the larger section of the loft. He needs it. His work consists mainly of these large assemblages . . . like big, black-canopied beds with motorcycles sleeping in fetal positions under shrouds of a liturgical purple satin. The market for such objects being rather slow as of late, he supplements his income by photographic portraits, and the sale of his hand-constructed jewelry. His necklaces, in particular, have become a hot item, being snatched up by the *très chic*, quack-honeys who lurk in Max's back room. Stuff like crucifixes covered in reptile skin: from his hands to Eurotrash necks.

The source of Jenny's concern . . . this "dreadful place" . . . stems from a trip the three of us made to Times Square last week. We three go up there frequently, proud to still elicit, in our post-teen years, the lurid howls of chickenhawks as we pass on by. Roger is unbearably pretty, touched by something sinister in his Egyptian eyes. I still look young enough to get proofed in bars . . . it must be my bangs . . . and, of course, I know *the walk* well from years gone by. Jenny Ann is amazing . . . she has breasts that are actually quite large, yet, *sans* bra, they hang, elusive and low, concealed in her oversized T-shirts; thus, she is mistaken constantly for one of the working boys.

We're not working, but we enjoy playing the part. We leer back at the viper-lipped suits with our desultory offerings, but keep moving on, and on. We weave through the crowds at Eighth Avenue, the air thicker there from the contrary breaths of evangelists and pimps. We hear the phantom sounds that still hang there from the ghosts of cheap, bright red radios . . . all the hits from all the charts . . . they've all passed by this corner and lingered in that thickened air, mixing now with the tinny reverb funneled through small, burnt transistors. This sound brings you to your knees like a sinner, and the preacher smiles mistakenly.

Something different every time. Tonight we find *that* place, right on Forty-deuce itself, between Seventh and

Sixth. It was one flight up. Roger led the way. He said he
hadn't been there before, but, in hindsight, I believe that
was a lie. It was a small room; it disoriented me as immediately as a paper cut. There was a single, old man there
behind a counter, plump in a seersucker jacket and over-
anxious to answer any and all questions concerning the
"exhibition." The exhibition, as it was, consisted of various
plastic molds of life-sized human bodies, at least two dozen
in all. They were *half*-bodies, actually, displaying the inner
organs, as in anatomy classes. But there was something
grotesque about these displays.

Each body showed the spreading of tumors, cancerous
tumors, upon certain vital organs. The halved-dummies
were sequenced in an order that showed, in hideous detail,
the effects of the cancer in progressive stages of growth.
The stout man ran all this down for us, caressing the fiberglass images, even removing, with a frightful snap, various diseased sections. He petted them as if they were ill
canaries, pointing out the effect of the growth of the tumor
on one particular organ. He went down the line, wrenching
out the lung from each dummy (he castigated me sharply,
as I recall now, for my use of this term "dummy," preferring to call them "representations") and shoving them up
into our faces. You could almost smell the advance of the
tumor on parade. Jenny and I had reached our limits by
the time we reached the twelfth "representation," politely
thanking our guide and tugging on Roger's shirttail. He
was not budging, especially when he saw the disappointment in the old guy's face. "But you've really only seen *half*
the exhibit," he whined, looking first at us, then turning
to Roger with a sharper urgency in his pleading stare.

Roger didn't even turn his head to us as he spoke, informing us in a tone which neither of us had ever heard
him employ before that he was staying, that he found it
fascinating, that we should leave straight off if we "couldn't
find any value to it."

Jenny was upset. She tried imploring him with a whimpering sound that was a language Roger alone understood. She had a similar means of communicating wordlessly with me, but at a different, somewhat higher frequency. Roger acknowledged the sound with a look of hostility, that sinister quality in his eyes breaking out to the forefront from its usual recesses. Jenny grabbed my arm in half-anger, half-panic, squeezing her long, thin fingers with a power she had never before revealed, even in orgasm. It was terror.

I snatched her hand and dragged her to the stairway; she had her head turned to Roger all the way to the door, continuing the whimper in an even higher, more urgent octave. When we reached the street, she bolted from me and ran to the curb to catch a cab that had already half-passed us by. It was then I realized the extent of her confusion, her anger and fear. We had a pact never to take cabs, and this anomaly shocked me. She burrowed into my chest. We didn't say a word all the way downtown, and wound up at my place instead of hers. She didn't want to see Roger when he returned. We fucked with the slow, long strokes that shut away fear.

When she *did* finally see Roger the next evening, he apologized and wept for the way he treated her. But he gave off no clues to his fascination with what Jenny and I had taken to calling, once she had settled herself, "The Cancer Hall of Fame." He didn't think our title very funny . . . nor the couplet I presented him with when I came over:

There is a rumor that this boy loves tumors
Enough to treat his friends with such bad humor

He even tossed it on the floor . . . an original manuscript . . . in my own hand, no less. "Well, the meter is flawed," I teased, "but, it *does* scan." He bugged out the door, slamming it, leaving a bunch of his reptilian necklaces bouncing nervously on a rack. I was sick of the whole situation, and told Jenny so. I mean, Roger is as susceptible and entitled to "the strange" as she or I. It's simply a matter of taste. The fact that his taste overlaps the truly tragic bizarro is really none of our concern.

But still, I had to hear it all again this morning, as with every morning this week, from Jenny, who was allowing herself to become a wreck over it. I reiterated my previously expressed analysis of Roger and his predilections. "But what about the sneezing?" she begged. I suggested that perhaps he was growing allergic to the plastic which composed the "representations." Jenny actually beamed. It was the best I'd seen her look in a week. She took me stone seriously. I stifled my grin and looked up to her, as if to say, "Well, there you go . . . that takes care of that." She rushed over, leaped onto the bed, stared at the ceiling a moment, leaving a flawless pause in her phrasing: "Yes," she spoke upward, "That would be the cure . . . that would be the eventual solution."

SUNDAY MORNING

I'm in need of dope, and I know just the place to find it. It's Sunday morning and I'm walking down Seventh Avenue with the sun just coming up and the street empty but for two deadbeats in from college for the weekend sleeping it off on the stoop outside a jazz club. I don't mind walking, next to taxis it's the best way to get there in New York City . . . so in an hour I'm ringing Palo's bell, fifth floor down the hall. His old lady, Lucinda, answers, though she's not a real lady by any means. Palo's old lady is a drag queen, a pretty, twenty-four-year-old Puerto Rican boy who prefers to dress like a woman. He pulls it off very well, so I like to give her the benefit of the doubt. She shares the apartment with Palo and another transvestite, Roselita. Roselita doesn't pull it off nearly so well as Lucinda, not nearly so well at all. It's all in the legs, I think, and Rosie's just don't make it. I don't give him the benefit of the doubt in any way, shape, or form. But I like Rosie well enough, and Lucinda as well. Palo, on the other hand, is a prick. If it wasn't for the efforts of the two ladies (sic) of the house, Palo would cut the dope to shreds. As it is, he's been stepping on it in ever-decreasing moderation, especially while the queens were away the last few months visiting relatives down in sunny Puerto Rico. Now that they're back, things have gotten better again. It's actually their operation and they have done very well by it. I'd have to take the "A" train up to the old neighborhood to get anything better.

Lucinda's purple mascara eye leans through the peep-hole and checks me out, long lashes like a trick spider. I hear a few muffled Spanish phrases as she undoes sundry bolts and locks and pulls open the door with the slow, justified paranoia of junk dealers. "*Es cool,*" she shouts back to the others and signals me in. Fortunately, Palo is on the heavy nod on the bed through a half-open door . . . if I'm in luck, they've just picked up a new shipment from up-town, and he's been too whacked-out from his taste test to step on it. Lucinda leads me to the sofa and sits me down between herself and Roselita. They're both in good humor, giggling in Spanish and flirting with me in that exaggerated, drag queen manner of flirt. They like me; they think my long, strawberry-blonde hair is something else. "I would trade you ocho ounces of ze fine-assed dope in thees city for my hair to be like thees," she always says to me, fingering it with her long, painted-blue nails. I go with the goof and flirt back this morning, since Palo is out of it. Otherwise, he actually gets uptight about guys responding to Lucinda's come-on, can you imagine? I mean, how can a guy who lives with two men in women's clothing be so lacking in a sense of humor? I tell them I want four for now, and Lucinda brushes into a back alcove to the stash. Rosie takes this as an opportunity of sorts and reaches over with a total lack of grace, subtlety, and, for that matter, conviction, and clutches my crotch. "I need uh man," she whispers. "Good luck," I reply, leaping up and half-noticing two pigeons fucking on the fire escape, "I hope you find one, Rosie." Lucinda comes back laughing, with four glassine bags in her hand.

"Wanna do it now?" she asks.

"Huh?"

"De dope, I mean," she clarifies.

I tell her I'm pretty straight as it is and I'd just as soon be taking off so I can catch High Mass around the corner at St. Agnes's in time for the Consecration. I hand her forty dollars, my little joke lost in translation, and split. I feel good hitting the streets in sunlight after all that squalor. I figure I'll walk home. I deserve a good nod. Passing St. Agnes's, I hear the choir voices pressed out the side doors by the organ and into the streets, stolen by the wind. I think about the line in Mayakovsky, *In the church of my heart, the choir is on fire.*" That's a junkie image if I ever heard one. I consider seriously for a moment actually going in and being part of it again. But I just raise my fingers to my forehead instead, and sign myself with the cross for old time's sake. And keep on walking.

TIMES SQUARE'S CAGE

I still recall, vividly recall, the first night I spent alone in Times Square. I followed this one whore through the late hours as she moved like a trawler through the currents of deals denied for short green. I was on her like a mutt puppy, always keeping a valve of safe retreat one quarter block long. I was more threatened by her than any stray pimps, who would, no doubt, consider me a heat-seeking pest at most. She was enormous, over six feet easily, including, naturally, her four-inch heels, which I thought inviolate . . . never to be removed. Her breasts were crawling, like some sea life from an unchartable depth, out of a black bra . . . the bra beneath a dress which was so short that, as I faked lacing my sneakers, crouching on one knee, I could clearly see revealed the connection of her black-

seamed stockings and her red garters, like two deadly circuits fused to activate a device of total annihilation. A vial
of mascara must have been emptied on those eyes. The
whole effect . . . the body . . . the dress . . . the makeup . . .
was as if someone had placed a Rubens portrait at the
bottom of a cesspool, and after centuries of strangeness
and decay among the stillness of vile things and vile notions,
some chance lightning hit . . . and out of it she was
risen . . . delivered onto these streets in a pink Cadillac.
And she walks and walks, because there is nobody who can
make her price.

That was a while back, but at least once a month I let
that desire out of its cage and swim through these sidewalks
like the sump canals of Babylon. You wear an erection with
the consistency of quicksilver, you breathe shorter breaths,
and even those grow quicker with the shadows growing
from side streets which are shaped for ignominy as a sports-
car is for speed. It's not like the periodic check-ins at a
clinic for the bemused, which I make with Jenny Ann and
Roger. You must be alone to achieve this wonderment, as
the others, passing by you, must be anonymous. That is
the key word. That is the sex which only the city allows.
God, there is nothing more downcast than running into
someone you know in Times Square. There can be no
external dialogue, only that between you and the iguana-
faced familiar you rented out at 42nd and Eighth. Otherwise, it's all a spiny silence; the fire engines' and cop cars'
sirens, the howls of the peep show boys, the threats of
cardboard preachers, either head off in another direction
or are devoured by the familiar, who spits it all out later
as something green and pink, in the shape of a baby bottle.

Whenever the thought arises, as it has lately, of giving
that small town in California, which my poet friends rec-
ommend constantly by mail, a chance, I must think of the
consequences of watching forlornly that desire for the quick
and anonymous, locked so long in its cage, evaporating like
an uncapped perfume. The horror of a town where every-

one knows your name, a town without humid side streets, without dangerous lust. Here nobody calls your name; they only point their finger, then move it, slowly but without caution, toward its own end.

THE PRICE YOU PAY

I fucked up. I sit here with my liver and kidneys vibrating inside from uncertainty in every direction. Poetry can unleash a terrible fear. I suppose it is the fear of possibilities, too many possibilities, each with its own endless set of variations. It's like looking too closely and too long into a mirror; soon your features distort, then erupt. You look too closely into your poems, or listen too closely to them as they arrive in whispers, and the features inside you— call it heart, call it mind, call it soul—accelerate out of control. They distort and they erupt, and it is one strange pain. You realize, then, that you can't attempt breaking down too many barriers in too short a time, because there are as many horrors waiting to *get in at you* as there are parts of yourself pushing to break out, and with the same, or more, fevered determination.

So you take what the muse gives, and try not to force it. You knock down one barricade at a time, making sure no more is behind them than you can handle, making sure they don't double up on you. You take drugs, perhaps, to calm things down but all the while you know that whatever poetry gives out, you must pay back eventually, with an incredible interest added on. Take my word for it, the muse, in one form or another, will be around to collect. The price you pay for drugs is a small pink simian who enjoys interlocking his twenty digits around your spine in a slowly tightening grip. But at least you are dealing with a pain fierce enough for you to understand, to endure. The subtle art of poetry carries a more subtle pain.

I shouldn't complain. When I say I "fucked up," what I mean is that I'm sitting here watching the NBA All-Star

Game on TV and I'm watching guys I used to seriously abuse on the court scoring in double figures now against the best in the game. Ergo, I fucked it up. I should have stayed an athlete, body well-tuned, cruising around with my accountant in a Porsche, maroon and chrome. More important, with basketball there's always only one direction: to the cylinder on the fiberglass rectangle. And you don't have to aim. If you do, you're off.

Poetry has too many variations. Mr. Frost was right about one thing: there are always promises to keep, and variations on that theme. With basketball you can correct your own mistakes, immediately and beautifully, in midair.

INVITATION TO THE DANCE

Of all the brilliant people I've met on the art scene, I suppose Edwin Denby is my candidate for the most interesting. He's rather old now, and looks even older because of his hair, which is a white the shade of moonlight. He isn't well known to the mass college audience as a poet, but he should be. The poets themselves, however, have great regard for his work. Frank O'Hara declared Denby to be one of his strongest influences. He's considered by many to be the greatest living critic of dance, both classical and modern, and his book, *Looking at the Dance*, is likely *the* definitive work on the subject. But what impresses me is that he has the most generous intellect I've ever come in contact with. I never pass up a chance to listen to him at a party.

I saw him the other night at one of Anne Waldman's gatherings and asked him about the story concerning the time he and Willem de Kooning were attacked by a butterfly in broad daylight on the streets of New York City. He explained that yes, the attack had in fact taken place. He had even written about it in one of his books. It seems this disoriented rogue butterfly, a rather large one, kept nipping at de Kooning's eyes. It was on Seventh Avenue

and 20th Street, right across from the building where Edwin
and de Kooning were neighbors in adjacent lofts.

"It would have been a strange ending to de Kooning's
career," I said, sort of giggling, "being blinded by a vicious
butterfly."

"It would have been a horrible tragedy!" Edwin spoke
solemnly in his slightly clipped European accent. It was
obvious he loved de Kooning as a painter and a friend.
"Such a great painter as he. But let me tell you something,
it was not so unexplainable an occurrence. You see, there
are certain species of butterflies which thrive on saline. It
is to them a great delicacy, as caviar to a man, or honey to
a bear. And where is there saline? In the eye, be it human
or animal. In South America, there is a species of crocodile
known as the Cayman. Perhaps you have heard of the
Cayman Islands? Well, wherever there are Caymans bask-
ing in the sun, on the bank of a river or swamp, there are
invariably hordes of butterflies flitting about the beasts' eyes
attempting to suck up the salty fluid. Sometimes the Caymans are so dazed by the sun that they are oblivious, and
the butterflies feast. Others move back into the water, where
they are still pursued by their winged parasites because
they must keep their eyes and snout above the waterline.
Eventually they are driven, these huge monsters which man
so fears, into their only sanctuary, the reeds and eel grass
growing out of the water. So you see, if these butterflies
can take on a crocodile, then why not a poor poet and a
painter on Seventh Avenue?"

I was astounded by the rap; so much so, that it prevented
me from asking if the little pest has escaped unharmed, or
if it was swatted down and squashed underfoot by a furious,
Dutch abstract expressionist. I'm glad I kept my mouth
shut because it gave Edwin the chance to invite me to a
preview of Balanchine's new piece at Lincoln Center the
following night. We set a time and place to meet, shook
hands and bid each other goodnight.

The next evening I entered the lobby of the New York

State Theater. Its elegance made me slightly anxious. I was ten minutes early for my meeting with Edwin, so I stepped outside onto the plaza. The air was sweet; it had that strange twilight temperature that betrays no particular season. I surveyed the complex of carefully lit buildings comprising Lincoln Center. "Mussolini-style architecture, like the Tombs down on Centre Street," I said to myself, though loudly enough for some pert coed tourist to hear me. She moved hurriedly away. I studied the giant murals done by Chagall flanking each side of the Opera House's lobby. They're fine as far as they go, but I always thought that the commission for those huge canvases should have been given to Hans Hofmann, whose work said so much more about the artistic energy of New York City.

I returned to the lobby and spotted Edwin's neatly combed white hair. I went up and greeted him, asking his forgiveness if I'd kept him waiting. He replied that he had just arrived, and then complimented me on my attire. I had, indeed, gone out of my way to look half decent, knowing how proper Edwin is. I knew that this jaunt to the ballet was Edwin's way of instilling some culture into my street sensibilities. I also knew that he enjoyed being seen at these events with good-looking young men (though it had more to do with their energy than their sexuality, and he certainly never made any advances to me), and for these reasons, I didn't want to embarrass him by showing up like some dirtbag. I was wearing my well-cut dress-up corduroy trousers (if they cost more than fifty dollars, I refuse to call them pants), and a matching velvet jacket, double-breasted with a quasi-Edwardian cut. It was very spiffy, if I do say so myself.

The jacket was a gift from my friend Bill Berkson. Throughout the sixties Bill was a perennial choice for the fashion magazines' "Best Dressed Men" lists, but sometime around '69, he grew his hair long and started giving away his fancy duds to his poet friends. It was an amazing scene. Bill was living uptown then, and you had these seedy poets

arriving at his apartment in their Goodwill threads and
then returning to the Lower East Side in breezy white Pan-
ama suits. I remember Ted Berrigan strolling barrel-chested
down St. Mark's Place wearing a Rudi Gernreich Nehru
jacket three sizes too small. As for me, I made out like a
bandit since I wore the same size shirt and jacket as Bill.
Bill's charitable gesture that day some two years ago made
it possible for me to look so resplendent as Edwin and I
were escorted to our box.

The beam of an elderly matron's flashlight directed us
to our seats. Edwin began chatting effusively with a regal-
looking couple beside him. Edwin promptly turned and
introduced us. It turned out to be the maestro himself,
George Balanchine, and his wife, who had that singular
charm that only comes from standing for years right beside
genius. The infamous "Mr. B." was positively aristocratic.
As the lights began to dim, I realized what an amazing
opportunity this was. I would be within earshot of the maestro's comments, seeing the ballet through his eyes as well
as Edwin's. It was fortunate that I had taken an amphetamine pill before going out. I was horribly embarrassed
when I nodded off the last time I went with Edwin to a
ballet. It would be even worse to fall asleep next to the
show's choreographer.

I wished that I knew more about dance, especially the
technical jargon, because I couldn't understand a lot of
what Balanchine was ranting on about. He was laying down
a running commentary from the moment the first pointed
toe made its entrance out onto the stage, his wife dutifully
taking notes on a steno pad. It was fascinating: his voice
had this tone of rage that made it seem like he was absolutely yelling. The fact is, however, that he was speaking
in a quite controlled whisper, not disturbing anyone around
us. I could only hear him because I was straining to do just
that.

He didn't have one positive thing to say. It was all a
stream of barbed invectives hurled at every dancer, from

the principals on down. He had an unbelievable ability to see the piece as a whole as well as to focus on each dancer's performance. When the last piece was over, and he and his wife had bid us a cordial goodbye, I was exhausted by all the detail I had taken in by daring to watch the dance through *his* eyes.

Edwin took me backstage. I was still somewhat dazed, but I certainly perked up when Edwin introduced me to my favorite *prima ballerina,* Patricia McBride. She had this radiant flush from just having danced and was even more beautiful up close than she was onstage. I had some ideas, especially when she seemed to pass the time allotted for perfunctory backstage greetings and actually began to converse with me, but I knew I was in over my head. Edwin gathered me off before I hyperventilated from the sight of all those tutu-clad dancers. It's true: I've always had a fetish for that gander-like walk, and the way they pin up their hair in buns, revealing those long-stemmed necks.

Once we were out on Broadway, Edwin and I stopped in a place for coffee, then said goodnight and parted in different directions. I made it over to the East Side to see what was happening at Max's.

I entered and headed for the back room. Things were kind of quiet, though Jackie Curtis was carrying on as usual with some friends in a back booth. Jackie is underrated at everything she does. I suppose she's best known as an actress and playwright, but she's got endless talents in other areas as well. Some people have this bias against her, thinking everything she does is based on a gimmick, just because Jackie is actually a man in drag. I don't call that a bias; I call it outright bigotry. I've spent many wonderful nights with her at Max's, as she's talked of her dreams of Scandinavia and a sex change.

"My God, Jim!" she spoke up as I approached her booth, "well aren't you all dressed up. A tie and everything! And that jacket! I never realized how *handsome* you were."

"Well, you know," I answered, feigning embarrassment, "I had to get all spiffed. You see, I went to the ballet."

"Ohhh . . . did you enjoy it? Was it wonderful?"

"Yeah, it was great."

"Didn't it make you horny? Everyone I know says the ballet makes them feel all horny. You should have some sex tonight, Jim. Really. You have to get laid after the ballet. It's a must! *Or at the very least, have a blow job.*"

That said, Jackie stood up and pushed open the rear emergency exit door that led out to the back alley. She took my hand and led me into the darkness, and then leaned me against the side of a dumpster. I made no real effort to protest, for whatever reason I don't know. Actually, her post-dance sex theory made some kind of frayed sense to me. Maybe I was just horny from the pill I'd taken earlier. At any rate, Jackie was down on her cheap-stockinged knees, humming the overture of *The Nutcracker* with her lips around my dick. My trousers were pulled down to my knees, and her hands ran up and down my thighs like disoriented mice. All I could think of, my eyes sealed tight, was Patricia McBride down below instead of Jackie. I think I even moaned out her name a few times: "Pat, oh Patti . . . let me do it to you while you're *en pointe.*" Jackie, meanwhile, was oblivious to my utterances. She had her skirt hiked up and was playing with her own dick while still sucking mine. I pulled away. It was a truly frightening scene. Jackie had a monstrous cock! The sight of it put a damper on all fantasies. I made myself as presentable as possible and returned through the rear door. Jackie followed me, asking what was wrong. Ha! As if she had to ask. Didn't she know how outright embarrassing it is for a man to get a blow job from a woman whose cock is bigger than his own?

A VICIOUS NOD

It was a rather baroque nod . . . something about a furious priest in one of those sack-like miniskirts chasing after me with a wooden stake and sledgehammer. I don't recall how it ended, but it's a good bet he caught me. *Something* very violent certainly went down. That was obvious by the pools of sweat retreating into the mattress as I bolted up; my shirt so soaked it was too much weight to bother removing. Then the blood. It was running down my chest, running rapidly, when I first saw it, through the damp crevices of cotton, breaking off across my thighs in all directions. It was almost a pink at first, mingling with the sweat, but the flow was so insistent it soon reached its own unmistakable depth of red. I just sat there, transfixed on the gradations of crimson settling in my pubic hair . . . some clotting there, most spilling off and into the mattress, following the sweat's lead. It was that spurt-driven flow which comes only from wounds which give off no pain, which give no clue to their source. The blood so busy, it is oblivious even to touch. If I cannot locate it through pain, I suppose I must check the mirror. The thought of actually making it visual . . . of granting its realness a final test, brings on a sense of horror so enormous it slices like hot screams through my thick narcotic stupor. I want to just sit . . . find another priest to race . . . but the blood won't quit.

I move quickly to the bathroom, holding a copy of Rilke's *Duino Elegies* under my chin to prevent red lines from forming on the plush, white carpeting. Is it my eye? Oh god, blood from the ears? My nose? Most people would think of the nose straight off, but I have never had a nosebleed in my life, truly. By the time I reach the tile floor of the bathroom, I have riddled Rilke's third Elegy with six violent stains, the worst having soaked through eight succeeding pages. I blot it with toilet tissue and slide it back across the carpet. The mirror. The mirror above the sink where I have begun to run both faucets, hot and cold. I stare a moment, eyes resisting what must be done. I toss a wash-cloth into the sink, then raise it up beneath the faucet marked "Cold." I use it less as a cloth and more as a means to lift up a full force of water, hurling it into my face. The blood abates a moment; I step backward until I hit the opened door against the wall, then move forward again. I scoop up another palmful of water and heave it again into my face, but this time I keep the soft square pressed intact. I can feel the sting as I probe fingers with varying pressure through the cloth. It is my lip . . . the sting repeats itself as I press harder this time . . . it is my lip. I'm certain. I pull away the cloth; the pressure and drainage of blood has left both lips the color of tainted salmon, pink and slightly blue. I realize that a sharp protruding tooth along the upper line has somehow pierced viciously through the lower lip, like a broken bit of china through a pink sponge. "Jeez," I muttered, "I wonder what that fucking priest *DID?*"

I was taking charge now, ready and somewhat able to practice some serious first-aid. I was humming a tune, in fact, I was so relieved . . . and humming with a hole in your lip is not an unpainful ordeal, I might add. All I could think of was this image of fountains of blood arcing out of both ears when I looked in that mirror, as if I were some gargoyle on the facade of a German cathedral. A hole in the lip? Bit of scar tissue? No problem . . . no problem, that is, until I hear a chorus of shrill, nubile female voices sounding off in circles behind my brain, "Oh my gawd . . . check out that geek with the *harelip.*" I pivot back around to confront the mirror again. I've dropped the humming . . . actually, I've just switched vocal dynamics, transforming it into a low moan. "It's not *that* bad," I console myself out loud. "It will mend through the processes which nature . . . no, no . . . which *God* . . . yes, which you, God, have given to man as a gift through your infinite wisdom and compassion . . . please. Amen."

My greater fears waylaid, I proceed again to the first-aid. I clean the wound with peroxide and a cotton swab, the soft breath of Morpheus blowing back the pain into some distant recess, where it waits to return later on with a vengeance. The blood totally stanched now, I examine the hole, a tattoo to the vague memory of an outraged priest. It was more like a slight tear in a gabardine-like garment . . . in the lapel, perhaps the result of the tense fingernails of an over-anxious lover. It was a small tear, but had, indeed, pierced through the entire lower lip. On a whim, I went over to the side table of the bed and grabbed a stray earring left behind by Jenny Ann. It was a series of tiny silver balls, five of them, descending in order of size. I inserted the loop through the pierced lip. It looked ridiculous. I toyed with the idea of wearing it into Max's tonight however, becoming a genuine trend-setter.

I checked out the tooth which must have done the damage. It was certainly sharp enough to perform such precise surgery. I had thought there was a pact between the body and brain to prevent such accidents within the dream state, but old Morpheus must have torn all that up. Or perhaps the tooth itself was a rogue, having broken away from its treaties. In the end, I knew the decay which formed such a dagger-fine point was due to nothing but my own neglect. I'm one of those types who never sees a dentist until there is something like a baseball-sized appendage within my jaw. I used to be an athlete; now I have become a contractor for decay. I began to think, as one only can when staring into a mirror, that the teeth were only the first to go . . . soon the rest of my body parts would begin making their own assumptions . . . calling their own shots. I seemed ten feet deep within the mirror as I thought, detached . . . as if my body itself was addressing me in total calm: "You have chosen to live so completely in your mind . . . in your dreams . . . in your nods, induced by such vile and toxic substance . . . well, look closely . . . your teeth . . . your torn lip which will soon, by the way, begin to swell to huge, ugly proportions . . . so you best remove quickly that ludicrous object you have inserted there to entertain yourself. Look well, and see what the results of such inane disregard can lead to . . . and it *will* get worse, you know . . . oh, much, much worse."

I moved out of the mirror, backed again to the door

pressed open against the wall, and slid to the floor, rubbing the blood in circles across the tile with my toes. I removed the earring and literally stuffed it into the toilet with one hand as I flushed it with the other. The silver balls didn't go down. I repeated the flush, over and over, but in the end they were still just lying there on the porcelain bottom, magnified slightly by the rules of liquids, the rules set down by nature.

THE POET AND THE VIBRATOR

I was dancing with Wren at Max's tonight ("Sympathy for the Devil"), waiting for my man (who happens to be a woman) to show with the ice, and the Velvets to come on at midnight, when I got a cryptic message from Anne Waldman, passed on by that blonde waitress who is always humming "Amazing Grace" and getting hit on by the parvenus of the quasi-Italian aristocrat set. Message read: "Hope you have not forgotten that the big "G" is in town for the night and that you said you'd put him up and that he will be at your apartment by eleven." I checked Wren's watch and, mild dismay, it was already ten past the designated hour. Of course, the big "G" was none other than Mr. Allen Ginsberg, and I recalled in one congealed mass of anxiety that I had indeed promised to put the great poet up since Billy B. (who allows me to share his place) was away in Mexico and Allen's apartment was being de-bedbugged by the fumigators this week and he was only in town for the night, en route from one university reading to the next, and, thus, I had to move ass back to 10th Street to allow him entrance and take the opportunity to engage him in deep poetic conversation. I told Wren hastily that I had to eschew any further *pas de deux,* and split, moving down Park Avenue South with post-dance floor exhilaration. I even forgot about the connection arriving with my goods . . . who cares about drugs when THE poet is waiting at your doorstep?

I turn the corner of 10th and Third to a comical scene: on an otherwise vacant street, darting glances left and right with the alacrity of petty crime paranoia, is the hirsute master himself, the leader of the pack, tossing pebbles from the street construction site down the block in handfuls against the window on the ground floor. "It's the window around back, you fucking juvenile delinquent," I whisper, having snuck up on his back with felony feet. "By the way," I add, "anyone ever tell you you throw like a girl?" He looks serious at first, then sheepish. "They just said it was the ground floor," says Allen, "I thought you might be on the nod or something."

"I never nod with the lights out," I shoot back, and we take the steps and I open the front door and lead him down the hall and into the apartment. It's a nice place, and a real steal to boot. Bill got it a year ago, furnished it with uptown money, and invited me to stay with him about four months ago. It has a loft for sleeping hovering over the small living room, a long hallway, and a cozy bedroom in the back, which also has a loft (used for stacking excess boxes of books, though the living room is lined with filled shelves already, floor to ceiling . . . you want to check out an allusion, then this is the place). I brew a little tea in the mini-kitchen off the living room while the "G" lights a spliff on the big velvet sofa. I usually pass on the loft, unless Deborah Duckster is staying over, and crash right there on the velvet luxury sofa. (I've yet to burn a single hole in it, I can proudly add.) I smoke the joint with Allen, get the bedding arrangements straight . . . "No, Allen, I don't think so, not tonight, etc." . . . I give him, instead, the honor of Bill's back bedroom. We get serious munchies and decide on Ratner's for soup and blintzes. Out into the energetic poet streets, Ginsberg getting the usual hippie cheers and blue-collar jeers. Half of America wants to look like him; the other half wants to see him dead. As for me, I see him eat . . . and, Lord, he can surely put it away. There's a little unscheduled floorshow in the back booths. It seems some big-time rock-and-roll concert promoter is telling Yippie leader Jerry Rubin that he is an asshole of enormous proportion. I asseverate this opinion of the promoter to Allen *sotto voce*. Allen, pressured to stick peer-assed to his fellow counter-Kulchur honcho, assures me what a lily Rubin, in fact, is. "Come on, Allen," I, in return, opine, "I mean, I dig Abbie in lots of ways, but Rubin is strictly from Robitussin—the best you can say is he's just a fucking placebo-ass, and, at the worst, he's dangerous hypocrisy in fancy boots . . . no shit, check out those feets . . . those rock-star snakeskin jobs goes for four hundred, at least. Give me a break." Allen begins to raise a finger, pedagogue style, but I'm rescued from the lecture by the arrival of dessert, which Allen obviously considers more serious business than the defense of Jerry Rubin.

On the way back home we run into none other than the abbot of Warholdom, Paul Morrissey. With his usual Bronx hand animation, he lays on Allen the outline of his newly planned project, a Civil War epic produced, naturally, by Andy, and directed by himself. He wants Allen to play the part of Walt Whitman, issuing aid and comfort, in every sense of the word, to the Union wounded (and any Rebels, for that matter, if they're cute enough).

"A lot of good-looking boys?" inquires Allen.

"That's the way we work . . . that's our signature, Allen," Paul replies..

"Sounds like fun," Allen is bubbling. "Any script written yet?"

"Umm, not yet . . . but we'll send it to you soon . . . an outline at least. By the way, Jim, maybe there's some work for you . . . like writing dialogue, when we get to that stage."

"Fine," I shoot back, "Just remember, any bones you throw me here and now will be picked up, stored away, and brought back to you later. So I hope you mean it."

"Don't worry," Paul assures me, "maybe we can even use you as a soldier. What about that, Allen? Don't you think that hair of Jim's would look nice in color on the screen?"

With that the conversation ended, and the abbot re-
sumed his manic pace, heading home to another night of
serious asexuality. I'm hoping his last remarks didn't in-
flame Allen's passion . . . turning the key into the apartment, I'm wondering what to do if he does try to put the
move on me.

After heating some tea and playing Allen The Who's
new L.P., I show him a new poem of mine in the recent
issue of *Poetry Mag*. He keeps mumbling things like, "You've
got some great lines here, some really great "haikus" within
the overall work, but what are you going to write when
they throw us in the concentration camps?" Terrific. Real
solid literary criticism. I could have gotten better poetic
advice from Leon Trotsky, for God's sake. I tell Allen to
speak for himself . . . I'm not planning on grabbing the bus
to the camps, myself. Fucking politics . . . I mean, does he
really believe it when he spouts that shit? Worse yet, could
he possibly be right? Have I not been paying attention
somewhere? Well, he *does* go on to make some more useful
comments, and they were quite generous, too. I like Allen;
I like to break down the solemn facade and reach the goof
heart. It's late now, and he gets off the sofa and asks again
where he should crash. There didn't seem to be any flir-
tatious inflection in his question, and I was relieved when
he put it in the singular "I" form. I tell him again that, as
honored guest, he gets to sleep in the master bedroom,
and lead him back there. As I'm setting the alarm clock
for Allen's early wake-up to get out to the airport, I hear
his voice behind me asking, "Hey, what's this thing?" I turn
around and gasp. In his hands the poet is holding Bill B.'s
heavy-duty, plug-directly-into-wall-socket-because-batter-
ies-are-not-enough-to-power-this-mother *vibrator*. I realize
that Deborah Duckster, the debutante, must have left it
lying right there on the sheets when she left yesterday
morning. It is a mean machine . . . three varying powers
and a hard rubber half-ball on the end. It probably gives
a hell of a body massage, but Deb and I wouldn't know

about that. The more-limited-area uses we have devised
for it, however, are spectacular. There is no way around
it; I explain to Allen its functions. As I detail the matter,
a great expression of sheer awe grows across Allen's face.
"You think I might try it?" he asks, his eyes bulging at the
intricacy of its engineering. "Be my guest," I tell him as I
walk back to the living room, "You better stick with the
low speed at first."

So as I lay down to read I hear the familiar hum of the
machine at its number one setting. Within minutes, nu-
mero dos . . . then the full roar of high speed. I hear a yell
from the bedroom, a big loud yell. "Holy shit," I jump up,
"his heart couldn't take it." I dash back. It's not a pretty
sight. Apparently, his scream was one of the ecstatic variety.
There was jism everywhere . . . he hit the bottom of the
sleeping loft above him, for God's sake. It was hanging
from a beam like a mini-stalactite. "Pretty good, boss," I
looked down, "that's what I call thrust." But The Poet had
a look of horror on his face . . . he was wrestling with the
vibrator like it was a fucking bobcat. It was still slapping
around his half-hard dick, which was red as a midget being
choked. "I can't turn it off," he burst out urgently. "Pull
the plug . . . quick . . . my dick feels like a sparring partner." I bent to the socket and yanked out the plug, then I
pulled it by the wire off Allen's spent body, as if I were
reeling in some lethal eel. There was some jism on the
rubber tip, but before I could grab a tissue to scoop it off,
it plunked onto the pillow next to the poet's head. "That
was incredible," he spoke in a sort of glottal stop, each
word popping from his lungs in a separate burst of air. I
didn't want to tell him (for fear he might want to try again)
that this was not the proper way to do it . . . that the right
way, at least to my mind, was to wear a pair of tight un-
derwear (I usually borrow a pair from Duckster) and run
the ball-tip along your hard-on as if you were ironing a
shirt. That way your cock doesn't whack around all over
the room and you're not left with cum hanging from every

shelf and rafter. I casually slipped the machine out of sight, then, offering another goodnight, retired to the sofa and my reading. Allen was asleep quickly, and I didn't hear either the alarm or him leaving in the morning. I found a sweet note on waking, however. Apart from other things, it said, "I hope I wasn't too much trouble . . ." Hardly.

ON GLORIA

Gloria Excelsior, one of Andy Warhol's superstars, has been hanging around the poetry readings at St. Mark's Church. St. Mark's is, of course, my home away from home. I guess it was Bill Berkson, my provider of room and board, who first brought her around. One night she stayed with Gerry Malanga after the reading and, in a moment of stoned blasphemy, got Gerry and me to pose naked on the altar, standing on each other's shoulders against the giant wooden cross. Gloria and I have been hanging about together, cross-lapping each other's grounds of operation, since that night . . . that's about a month, a full month.

Gloria is a speed freak, in the true sense of the word. She has been on a virtual nonstop run of speed, in one form or another, for the last ten years. You'd think she'd have wasted into one of those arcane, babbling exclamation points with shoes by this time. The fact is she has to be, let's not mince words, the fattest speed junkie in the history of pharmaceuticals. If she's five-foot nine, then she is at the very least 240 pounds, and that's a kindness on my part. On the other hand, I've lost close to twenty pounds in the last month. Gloria has talked me into undergoing her therapy to cure me of my addiction to heroin, a drug she genuinely despises. This therapy of hers involves constant injections of methedrine in any form possible. The favored form is dysoxin in these 15 mg. pills. The pills are actually nothing but rounded bits of plastic with a yellow dust of pure meth. One simply takes thirty or so of these little gabbers, leaving them in their little pill bottle . . . she does get these things from a legit drugstore, I've discovered . . . and fills the vial with water, leaving it to soak overnight, and wakes up the next morning to find a jaundiced liquor, suitable for injecting. The pills just sit there on the bottom of the bottle, a bone-white color now, but, in every other sense, undissolved. I can't imagine what they must do to a person's stomach if swallowed as directed. They look like tiny skulls through the yellow haze of the solution. Be that as it may, it is a potent solution indeed. I take it straight in the vein so as to get the maximum rush, which is something like inserting a model railroad locomotive into your bloodlines and having it run, at open throttle, directly from armpit to heart to brain, proceeding on to local stops everywhere else in the body after delivering to these prime points. The trouble is that, of late, I smell circuits burning somewhere in the tracks. Gloria seems to go on in stride, urging me to force myself to eat. I don't want to eat. I want to talk. I talk to everybody, and it pisses me off when they interrupt to talk back. I sometimes think of offering money to friends to buy their turn in a conversation.

And we talk on the phone. It's Gloria's art form. She tapes every telephone conversation in and out of her room at the Thomas Jefferson Hotel. Her room is like the brain of a perverse child. There are little furry things everywhere. She lies on her bed and cuddles them in a fetal position (which, at her weight, is quite a sight) and talks and talks. The place is only about ten by ten. She has every inch of every wall covered with some kind of art or curio. Some of the works are fantastic . . . all the biggies—Andy Warhol, Jasper Johns, Bob Rauschenberg, are represented. But it's all so crammed together that it just melts into one abstraction with a feeling of vertigo. Especially with this particular drug: it's like standing out on a ledge twenty-three flights up, alone with the attraction of the zenith. She also has a collection of vibrators that must run up half the electrical wattage in the hotel. Sex within such a confined space couldn't, by the laws of physics, be anything but bizarre. And it is. Did you ever play lamp? That's all I'm saying.

THE ART OF USING

Regarding Gloria's artistic endeavor, which consists of tapping her telephone calls, I might mention that Warhol does this as well. When I say "as well," I do not mean it in a qualitative sense, since it is difficult to distinguish merit when using such a medium. I'm not coming down on it; the premise is really not that different, in an abstract way, from that used by two of my artistic heroes, Jackson Pollock and Frank O'Hara, the former with his drip canvases, the latter with his book of lunch poems. That is, the act of creating the piece and the finished work become one and the same . . . the subject and object meet, as the sky and sea meet to form the line of horizon, the point of reflection. I used to go to the beach and stare at that line all day, in the blue clarity of winter. Winter defines the passage of the earth and its forms better than any other season, as if the cold froze each frame of moving film. I can stare at Pollock or read Frank's poems all day. But I can't stand another moment of listening to these fucking tapes Gloria is always playing me when I show up at her room and all I want is to rattle speed into my shaft.

The distinction is simple. With Pollock or Frank, it was the private struggle from within which created that incredible tension, the drama of their human voices overlapping, the forces of their wills conflicting . . . with grace or complete vulgarity. With phone-taping the "art" is dictated totally by the merits of the conversation. Sure, it can be funny or interesting for a while, but eventually it's always going to be boring. That's because it is, by the nature of the medium, bereft of the privacy which is essential for that conflict, that struggle of forces to ignite into something beyond itself. It's all on the surface, like Gloria's other art form, the Polaroid picture, another obsession of Warhol's.

I don't know for sure who gets these notions first, and I'm sure if it was Gloria's idea, the fact that he does it also doesn't matter at all to him. To me, it's like jerking off instead of fucking, and that's not all . . . it's worse than that. It's like jerking off and coming so quickly that the fantasy is not only unfulfilled, but never even has time to formulate itself. I can remember when you had to wait an entire sixty seconds before the Polaroid ejaculated the print . . . then it was thirty . . . then it was ten. Now it's fucking instantaneous. I mean, talk about premature art.

But it's the phone-taping that's truly insidious—not only is it not private, it is an intrusion. It is FBI/CIA art. Imagine the gallery those dudes could open—I'd pay to hear Martin Luther King talking to J. Edgar Hoover, with Hoover sitting in his office in drag pretending he's a hooker. Somebody is always at the other end of the line, unaware that the machine is running, and that the little suction cup is planted on Gloria's receiver, devouring every word.

For that matter, what difference does it make if both parties . . . why do they call them parties, anyway? I'm always calling someone in desperation . . . know and understand they are being recorded? Andy calls here twice a day and, since he knows we're both whacked on speed, Gloria and I, he milks us of every prefix and suffix of gibberish we have in us. Gossip is the bulwark of Andy's art. He has a reel-to-reel of every conversation for the last seven years. He doesn't even bother to play them back . . . an idea I wish Gloria would consider, at least when I'm around. But she thinks I am seriously interested in hearing every word of banal bullshit which Peter fucking Beard had to say to her that morning. I'm on a drug that makes you want to talk, not listen, for Christ's sake.

Andy just called, in fact. That's where the impetus (lest I say inspiration) for this piece comes from. He woke me up . . . Gloria is out at the coffee shop proving it really is possible to shoot speed and eat fourteen cheeseburgers within the same twenty minutes . . . and, realizing I wasn't stoned on that bullshit drug, he didn't have a word to say. Usually he won't allow me to consider getting off the line for half an hour, but I'm not of any use to him in my natural sublimity. He just told me how butch I sounded when I had just woken up and proceeded to sever the connection. I feel like a fucking handkerchief just back from the laundry—nobody's interested in you if you're not filled with snot.

A NEW JOB

I've been spending a lot of time up at Andy Warhol's studio, known better to the faithful as "The Factory," doing odd assignments for short money. Andy is a tough man (sic) with a buck. Today I had to come up with a list of thirty names for characters in a new play he's orchestrating for a show in Europe, tentative title "Pork." I sat in a corner overlooking Union Square Park and watched the passing of continental types visiting, checking out their routines (Andy really can bring out the asshole in a person) and laying a name on each. There was this sporty Italian type, hands constantly fingering a Gucci ascot, and the name "Cosmo Pugio" jumped onto the page. A seedy type from the land of the rising sun popped in, looking like he had a cache of automatic weapons waiting downstairs in the sidebags of his Kawasaki. What else to call him but "Itinki Soonkum." Turns out he was an interior decorator trying to unload a van-full of Bonsai trees on A.W. to give the place that sylvan touch. After thirty of these aficionados and parvenus passed in and out, I had my list.

Everyone thinks The Factory is constant orgies and Marlon Brando coming in just to say hello, but the truth is it's boring as an empty bag and the only celebrity I've seen in the past two weeks has been fucking Donovan, for Christ's sake. Of course, everyone who graces these portals is a "star," but their fifteen minutes were up long ago. The old Factory up in the West Forties was actually a wild scene,

but since Andy took a bulldyke bullet in the rib this place
has about seventeen doors on the elevator, a receptionist
who was no doubt an abused child and takes every opportunity to even it up, and security cameras running up the
ass. It's also kept immaculate. The floors are these parquet
jobs that outshine the Boston Celtics' home court. The
desks are glass on chrome high tech, papers stacked in neat
piles on tops filled with electric Rolodexes, Princess phones,
staplers that look like they were designed by German ar-
chitects, sleek IBM Selectrics, and what look like Waterford
crystal jars for paper clips. Everything appears great, but
I couldn't imagine typing on glass. On the other side of a
teak partition wall is a huge screening room with tastefully
curved sofas and deep pile carpeting, white as a virgin polar
bear. There's not much art hanging . . . just some of Andy's
works in the back recesses of the screening room, his "work
space," though nobody's made an effort lately to fulfill that
title. There's a stuffed German Shepherd with a hard-on
mounted and placed near the elevator. I'm not sure if it's
art or a security decoy.

CURRENCY

Actually, I shouldn't bitch about this gig up at Warhol's.
It gives me time to type up poems in impressive typeface
and, the truth be told (for at least one time up here), I like
Andy. Despite Paul Morrissey's strict anti-drug edicts, I'm
kept on as long as I wear long-sleeved shirts.

I think I understand how this operation works. It's all
so on the surface that everything just slides along. It's like
rain on a tin roof, or air raising up one of Andy's silver
helium pillows. The feelings are so shallow that there never
is time for drifts to accumulate and slow things down. Even
the boredom has no depth; it's just a stamped impression
of the continuously subdued. The poles are greased so
thoroughly with bullshit and artifice that depth hasn't a

chance. You look at the faces . . . two-dimensional, as if each had somehow leapt off newly pressed dollar bills. The only thing that separates one from another, the hierarchy from the hangers-on, is the denomination. Ultra Violet and the other "superstars" are just so many used-up singles, easily burned up in a sporting moment. Truman Capote is a pill-stained thousand. The wife of a shah—well, that's Woodrow Wilson on a one-hundred-thousand dollar bill. But they slide so easily together, and with the slightest wind they'll all lay together, heaped on the parquet floorboards.

THE CYCLE

After another day and night of dysoxin-methedrine injections with Gloria, followed in the later hours by palmloads of seconal barbiturate, previously and herewith referred to as "reds," I woke up on the floor of Gloria's mini-hotel room shortly before noon, to the sound of determined footsteps from a passing caravan of gypsy roaches. I watched with a single eye open, body still, until they had completed their nomadic drive through cracked varnish, chaparral-like tufts of dust and tight curls of stray pubic hair, finally disappearing through a crack beside the radiator pipe.

It's not that I am protective of vermin. I had the *Times* from last Sunday within my reach and, normally, out of city-bred compulsion, would have leveled them into shred and slime with the book review section, which I've always found has the precise weight and flexibility to handle the job more efficiently than, say, the more cumbersome Sunday Magazine. No, I allowed them safe passage for quite a different reason. The fact is, I was just not prepared for the consequences if, on completing the assault, I was to discover that they, to put it straight, did not really exist outside the drug-ravaged confines of my brain, which has been rapidly turned into a side dish searching in vain for the main course. So, if these bugs were nothing more than

the proverbial figments of some cooked circuit above my
neck, I was not quite ready to prove it to myself at that
specific time. It might mean I'd have to reconsider injecting
the drug, which I had just drawn up from the ampoule,
into my vein, and considering the hangover from the barbiturates, that would be too harsh a discomfort to confront
on a weekday noon.

   You see, what we have established here, Gloria and I, is
your classic vicious cycle. One continues to inject the speed
throughout the day for energy, dubious insight, and social
interaction. Show me someone who's not stoned in this city
and I'll show you someone with a well-worn television set.
So after ten or maybe, as the old tolerance adjusts itself,
twenty more repetitions of the ritual, one starts to feel a
bit, well, nettled by evening . . . so it's time for a few Valiums. The night comes, the shots continue, as do more
Valiums, and you come to the point where you realize that
it has been three days now without either food or sleep.
You force down a cheeseburger, or some broiled shrimp
at Max's, and you decide that this novelty known as sleep
might be worth trying—it seems that everyone's doing it.
You're in luck because you notice that two booths over in
Max's back room happens to be Rip Van W. (nobody's been
able to find out what the last initial stands for), and he has
a bagful of variegated little capsules that, when pressed out
flat on the glass table top and lit from beneath, look like a
collaborative painting done by Frank Stella and Larry Poons.
The red ones are just what you want for your problem . . . wait, no . . . we don't like that word . . . let's make
that your "situation." And it is truly amazing, the way, after
all that meth you have inflicted on yourself throughout
three entire days, it takes only two of these pills to send
you right off to sleep. And it goes on like this for a week,
but now, instead of two of these red pills, it's suddenly
become seven or eight. Conversely, you need more speed
in that first wake-up shot, a more condensed solution, so

to speak. And, of course, I use the word "solution" in a strictly pharmacological sense.

And here I am—filled with my solution, strong enough and filled with enough energy to make any vow, to break any vow, to break my staff, bury it certain fathoms in the earth. But break the cycle, just when I'm seeing insects that may not be there? Just when the circle has completed itself, as if to form a shield for my boring cynicism? Just when my analogies are arriving . . . just when the snake, coiled and tired, is about to devour its own tail?

NEW ACCOMMODATIONS

This morning I left my house-sitting stint at Bill B.'s apartment on 10th Street and checked into the summer accommodations that Gloria has arranged for me. Quite as elegant a place as my needs require. Certainly beats jackshit out of that Tijuana suite I was holding down off and on at the Chelsea. It's mainly one big room, with a decent-sized kitchenette, set off by one of those counter-with-bar-type-stool numbers—the spot where the wife serves orange juice and coffee in haste to the dutiful husband who has to make a dash for the office. "No time for eggs, dear. No, not even toast. I've got that damn presentation this morning, and I've got to get in early to go over some last details with Arnie and Stu." There's also a neat little guest room with a single bed off to the side.

I like to allow a new place to dictate itself to me and to determine the way I approach the actual functioning conditions of living there. I can never bring myself to change a thing from the way it was when I first walked in. I accommodate it, not vice versa. When I was a child, I always imagined that if the furniture were unhappy with the way it was arranged, it could always switch itself about to suit its needs and whims at night under cover of darkness.

One morning when I was about four years old and just

recovering from a serious fever, my bed had moved from beside my brother's bed in one corner across the room to right beneath the window. For the first time I enjoyed the morning breeze on waking. I could hear the muffled coo of those tubercular pigeons on the fire escape and, naturally, I assumed the bed itself enjoyed these things as well and had taken it upon itself to remedy the situation. I was indignant when my mother tried to take credit for the rearrangement and refused outright to accept my idea.

So I leave things as they are . . . piously. To me, interior decorators are the scum of the earth. There are only two exceptions to my rule: I do take the liberty of changing the angle of televisions and fans if it is absolutely required. Amazingly, however, the TV here is in direct visual line with the convertible sofa in the living room which, fortunately, has already been folded out and dressed with clean linen by Gloria. That's good because I refuse to convert sofas and I'd much rather sleep on this queen-sized mattress than that dinky job in the tiny room. Needless to say, it will not be converted back until I depart the premises. Here is some wisdom: A room is always perfectly capable of working things out for itself.

TRANSFER— MOVING UP, DOWNTOWN

I don't know if I should think of it as a promotion or a demotion, but the fact is that, although I remain on The Factory payroll, I'm no longer working at my corner desk up at Studio della Warhol. I think it was Paul Morrissey who engineered the move, but it's of no consequence with whom the edict took shape. I'm just glad to be out of the confines of that fortress, free from having to run down fifteen code words for each entrance door every morning, fearing to commit the slightest manual communication with my crotch under the scrutiny of zoom lenses from four angles. Actually, that might explain, jest and hyperbole aside, why all the desktops are glass—better to spot the next subversive employee molding plastic-explosive statuary under his desk in a fit of serious disenchantment. It wouldn't register on the metal detector, and it would certainly be no problem to roll it into some oblong configuration, stick a piece of lucite beneath it and mount it on a windowsill in Andy's office under the guise of minimalist sculpture.

I suppose you could label my new assignment "field work," since my new location is 3rd Street, right off the upper Bowery. The job: co-manager (with Gerry Malanga) of a boy-beaver movie house operating under Andy's name. Andy's actual participation in this is, as usual, next to nil. He simply lends his name to the theater itself and to the advertising in the dailies and the usual underground rags. It's misleading, naturally. Some aficionados come down expecting the films to be (can you imagine the nerve?) actually *made* by Warhol himself. Truth be told (watch out), all one gets for the five-bill admission is an assortment of the same boring porn loops shown up in Times Square for three dollars less. It's all that accountant-meets-cowboy, muscle-beach-bop-in-the-surf shit that they churn out on the West Coast at the rate of four miles of celluloid a day. I've been here a week now, however, and only one arty type has complained thus far, claiming that the likely conclusion from the ads was that these were going to be films by the master himself. I asked him whether they turned him on or not. He considered this a moment, stroking his icy cheeks and replied, "Well, yes . . . I mean the boys were pretty and all, of course, but . . ." I cut him off on that note, however, and informed him that there were absolutely no refunds. He didn't argue the point and, in fact, smiled rather sweetly as he turned to track some young blood who was making a hasty exit to our left.

WHO WILL BE
ACCOUNTED FOR?

My title of co-manager of "Andy Warhol's Theater: Boys
to Adore Galore" (or AWT-BAG as we call it from the
inside) is a somewhat strained euphemism. There's actually
only two people handling each shift: the projectionist, my
man Tiny Tommy, and me. I take care of the ticket booth,
i.e., I take the money, hand the patron a ticket and point
to the staircase leading up to the seats. This demeaning
task does not encompass my notion of managerial duties.
And I thank the Lord above each day that this is the case;
I wouldn't have it any other way.

You see, what we have here is a goldmine of free-
enterprise opportunity. Since there's nobody else down here
to *take* the tickets after I issue them, which is the standard
operating procedure in any other movie house I can think
of, porno or Walt Disney, there is no real way to account
for the number of people who actually enter. Of course,
there is the machine that is used to punch up the tickets,
and I am always quite careful about making note of the
ticket number which starts and ends the shift. Naturally,
the tickets in between are numbered in sequence, thus giving an accurate count of just how many customers pass
through these pleasure portals. And this satisfactory ac-
counting is exactly what our fastidious abbot gets when he
comes to pick up the money box each night at closing.

But it occurred to me right after assuming my duties as
manager-ticket boy, that if you just take the admission price
(which I regard as outrageous) from, say, every third or
fourth customer, discard the tedium of punching up a
ticket, stick the fiver in your pocket, and simply motion the
person upstairs with a blasé wave of the index finger, then
you can find yourself holding as much as two or three
hundred dollars in that pocket by the time the abbot makes
his rounds at midnight. It's especially easy on Tuesdays
and Thursdays, which are the days the feature is changed,

because the place is filled up with the faithful who never doubt that the next one is going to provide the ultimate under-the-raincoat orgasm.

The way I view it, with those bloated admission prices, it's only just. And, though I can't be certain about this, I believe I am backed in this hustle by holy scripture. I mean, didn't it say somewhere in that most illuminated of texts something along the lines of: "And I say unto you, not all shall be accounted for"? Wouldn't the abbot himself approve? Besides, those peckers are making out like bandits on this arena of obscenity. And I am, after all, the manager.

ROBERT SMITHSON DOES SOME IMPRESSIVE TALKING TO AN IDIOT WHO JUST TRAILED A BEAM OF LIGHT

From this apartment which Gloria has gotten me for the summer, only a few doors over from Park Avenue South on 22nd Street, it's become a nightly routine to walk down to Max's to meet Gloria, hear the Velvet Underground (who are playing upstairs twice a night, six nights a week), or just hang out in the back room. On my way there tonight I realized just how clever this unknown conceptual artist is—the one who designed the laser beam that runs seven blocks in every odd direction, winding up, finally, on the wall in the backroom of Max's itself. I've always picked up its path as I turned the corner onto Park South at Twenty-deuce, but tonight, feeling quick and energetic, I resolved to trace it to its source, something which no one has been able to do. The night was perfect for my enterprise, the darkness clear and with a blue sharpness. I picked up the beam, red and beautiful as a tube of liquid roses, in the usual spot and began to backtrack from there. On 23rd Street I noticed that it turned, heading off a mirror five flights up a building facade on the southwest corner, in the direction of Lexington Avenue. With my eyes glued to its steady flow, I got all the way down to Third Avenue before it turned again, this time broken by a more complex mirror which split the beam into two equal parts, one going up-town, the other going downtown. I guessed that the down-town beam was the proverbial red herring, so I traced the uptown one two more blocks, where it split off the side of a warehouse wall (right out of the mouth of a gargoyle there . . . it was genuinely eerie) into four other directions, including one that, with the aid of another mirror across the street, sent one of the lines into two more parts, one of which went back in the direction I had come, this time on the other side of the street. I was ready, however, to match my determination with its creator's considerable wit, and I ran back down to 23rd to follow the downtown light from where it had originally split in two. That was of no use either; it simply went down two blocks, shot off the angle of a mirror pointing back west and, passing Gramercy Park, went right back over to Park Avenue South at 21st Street, reuniting with the original beam . . . one block from where I started this glamour-filled quest.

Staring up at it with a slumped posture which read de-jection, I heard a voice whisper, "Forget it. I'll buy you a drink at Max's . . . at least you'll see where it ends." It was Robert Smithson, the earthwork artist—one person who frequented Max's for whom I had total respect in every sense: intellect, taste, heart. We invariably loved the same movies, and that was usually the source of our conversa-tions. His reputation was growing lately by leaps and bounds, and he was in the process of knocking off his masterwork—a spiral configuration of many-colored stones in the shal-lows of the Great Salt Lake. I greeted him, still a bit dazed from being led around by the nose by a beam of red light.

"It's just a labyrinth," he spoke in his subtle, likeably erudite voice, "and like those libraries in medieval clois-tered abbeys, it is a labyrinth which is not supposed to be penetrated. So give it up." I noticed a serious tone to his voice, almost of warning.

I explained that those libraries were constructed, with great genius, as labyrinths because the abbots in those times were in genuine fear of the wrong kind of knowledge reaching the novices or, for that matter, reaching anyone beside the abbot himself and his appointed librarian. What, then, was the analogy he was making? After all, all one would find at the other end of the laser was some artist's studio with a contraption filled with various gases—most likely, since it was a red beam, krypton.

"That's it," he picked up on the cheap pun, "krypton . . . why it must lead to Superman and his fortress of solitude."

"I see we have the same tastes in literature as we do in cinema," I said. "But, no shit, do you know anything about where it leads? And why are you so serious?"

"Because," he answered, getting a bit weary of all this, I noticed, "like those superstitious monks, this artist, whoever he is, is harboring secrets as well . . . maybe great secrets or, perhaps, just the fears inside his own head, not so different from those abbots and their fears. He might fear fame, though I don't see, clever as this thing is, what he has to sweat about."

"You smug prick," I laughed.

"The point is, we don't all of us want fame. And, the way things are going in my life lately, I can understand his point. It's as much of a trap as following around this fucking beam of condensed light." He pointed up. We stared a minute, then followed it to its end where we sat and had a drink of Pernod and beer. You heard me right.

THE ABBEY

I've been playing constantly with the conversation I had with Smithson the other night, and I realize the analogy of an artist's loft as a medieval abbey fits Andy's Factory like white on rice. It's especially true since the master came within a centimeter of buying it with that bullet. These are cloistered walls, secure from all except, perhaps, those who might increase the coffers with gold or art. A soup can on canvas is not so very different from a reliquary of precious stones stripped down by the dealers in a marketplace.

Andy himself doesn't fit in as the abbot-head. He is more like some pope in exile, given sanctuary here after offending the empire. He hovers about, giving his blessing to the novitiates' good work with one hand and extending his ring with the other, usually to the envoys of wealth and power. He accepts commissions rather than handing them out; the switch is simply a concession to his own century. Beneath the head man, as in any abbey, the pecking order begins. Wide-eyed novitiate that I am, I can speak without malice. And I, as all others within these confines, yield to the abbot, to his formal interdictions and his casual whims. The abbot, who plays his part in this analogy better than all others, surely must be Paul Morrissey.

Paul Morrissey is one of those most dangerous of creatures—a Bronx Irish Catholic who transcended his surroundings just enough, while partially maintaining the essential qualities of his white ghetto upbringing. Born of the trepidation and frustration of that mentality, these qualities are political and moral ultraconservatism, firm yet unaligned bigotry, and a pitiable sexual fear. When I say that he transcended this environment just enough, I mean that, having reached college and certain academic standards, he would always pull up short. He settled for cleverness and cunning, totally forsaking vision. He was content with the detail, rather than the wisdom, of any given knowledge. The aesthetic was totally disregarded for the pragmatic. In short, he chose advanced business and management over his shot at illumination, all the while sucking in like ether the psychological paraphernalia of success across the tracks—well-formed manners, an energetic personality, and the art of kissing serious ass. I knew a lot of guys like him, but very few as skilled. I know him like I know my own self and my own brother, and the severed ends in between.

By the same token, he knew me. And, like a confessor who knew this novitiate's hidden lusts and failings, he tolerated me with a like-neighborhood style and humor. For one thing, I was in a constant state of disobedience toward the prime edict: no drugs. He was fanatical on that score, as on others. Not content with his duties as abbot, he doubled as Grand Inquisitor. It was Gloria's intercession that kept me around. She assured him I was off heroin. And I was. I was simply substituting it with twice as much speed which, as I have so often opined, leaves H in the dust as one runs the race of self-destruction. No doubt Paul knew all about Gloria's using, but she was an old-timer at the abbey and a strong off-hours comrade of Andy's, so Paul wisely let it lay, knowing he had a ways to go in consolidating his power. He had just expended close to all the energy and cunning he could muster from his bag of tricks in overthrowing my poet chum, Gerry Malanga, the former abbot, to whom our exiled pope owed much of his acclaim, and there was no way he was going to expose his other flank in a move against Gloria, no matter the extent of her drug heresies.

I'm watching him at this very moment. He's good. He even looks like an abbot—gaunt, sinewy and slightly bent. With the energy of his movement, one can easily imagine a robe—plain, functional and brown—flowing from his body with the sheer speed of his motion, which is continuous and preconceived, always the shortest distance between two points. It's amazing how the part fits. I might as well be illuminating some sacred tome in the scriptorium of a great library instead of sitting here at a glass desk writing veiled porno dialogue for my superior's next presentation. He exudes the primary qualities of many ordained shepherds: the greed and the work ethic of a Benedictine, the contempt and staunchness of a Domini-

can, and the harshness and discipline of a Jesuit. I sometimes wonder about the nature of his devotion to Andy, if
it is pure or selfish, another means to another end. I don't
know the answer. I do know this much: like any young
monk in any given abbey, I feel its continual sense of in-
trigue, and confess to the pleasures therein.

A PECULIAR-LOOKING GIRL

A peculiar-looking girl, about nineteen years old, picked
me up this evening while I was making a phone call in the
booth near the men's room at Max's. I couldn't quite put
my finger on the exact nature of this peculiarity, but she
definitely had a problem with her posture. She also kept
telling me, in this giggly voice which was totally without
appeal, sex or otherwise, that I looked a lot like Iggy Stooge,
the rock and roll trashmaster. If that was supposed to be
great, I couldn't figure out why. She had this annoying
habit of rolling her eyes around the top of her head when
she spoke, like a ventriloquist's dummy, which made anything she said immediately forgettable and irritating. I had
only stopped in there to partake of the free Friday evening
happy-hour hot plate of chicken gristle and bad chili. It
was still evening, still light out on the streets as we split for
her place. I checked the twilight on Park Avenue South
for signs of the laser, which still haunts me like a bad lot
of LSD, but there was either still too much day left for it
to make itself manifest, or Dr. Strange hadn't turned it on
yet.

   Her apartment was only about seven blocks away, but
that was far enough for me to already be having second
opinions about the whole idea. By the time we were crawling up the shaft of her freight elevator (she lived in a loft)
my second thoughts had turned into a positive doubt. She
kept babbling on and rolling her eyes around. By the time
we were entering her place, a large, low-ceilinged shambles,
I had completely re-evaluated the situation and realized it

was simply a move made in haste without much taste and
it was time to get wasted. Before anything whatsoever happened.

Luckily, she made a contribution toward my chance for
salvation, telling me she was going to have a bath first since
she'd been out all day. By the tone in her voice I could
discern she was intimating that it would be a great thing
if I would join her. Not, I believe, that she was coming on
for aqua-coitus but just because she thought it would be a
sound and novel idea in the way of personal hygiene, mine
as well as hers, if I scattered a little warm water over my
body. I told her to go ahead with it, that I'd relax on the
couch and wait. She grimaced and went off.

When she was in the other room with the water running
I reached into the inner lining of my suede coat and retrieved a Band-Aid box which contained a new twenty-
seven pt. syringe, a bottle cap, cotton and four three-dollar
bags. It was from a new connection and was supposed to
be a hot property. I filled up a glass by the sink, threw in
two bags and began the procedure. I was just finishing up,
the needle still in the vein for one last boot down the old
line when, wouldn't you know it, she appears in a fucking
kimono at the far end of the place. I can imagine the chump
smile on my face, snagged in this outstanding act of vulgarity when I should be taking a bath. But it's strange, she
doesn't act alarmed at all. If she's that blasé and accustomed
to it, I figure, you'd think she'd at least ask for some. She
just goes into a dresser and pulls this box out of a drawer—
it looks like hippie bathing oil or bubble bath or something
along that line—smiles down at me, asks again if I'm sure
I don't want to join her, and continues back to the bathroom. I come to realize, despite an incredible rush of mor-
phia bliss running through my body during her entire
appearance, that she must have had her contact lenses out
and was blind like Milton from such a distance across the
loft and, in fact, never saw a damn thing.

I wish I could say the same thing because I had seen,

directly through the watering in my eyes, exactly what it was that made me think of her as peculiar-looking. As she bent over the dresser, I could plainly see through the sheerness of her kimono that she was a hunchback. And I'm not talking about a small protrusion here. I'm talking serious hunch, as in hump, as in Notre Dame.

I was shocked. I was also quite ripped out of my mind. The word on this dope was no exaggeration. I thought I should take advantage of her being submerged and make for the elevator, cleaning up my works and the blood off the floor, where I had coyly dumped it before I realized she was Quasimodo's blind daughter. While I was trying to decide on this course of action, however, the dope really kicked in and I collapsed into a nod which I don't totally recall, though I do remember that Friar Tuck and Sherlock Holmes were in it, riding in a mobile home with me through the main street of Southampton. Tuck wanted to stop and buy a polo shirt, but Holmes, deft at the wheel, refused to pull over.

When I came to, the place was in total darkness. The girl was dragging me across the floor, kicking me in the side with pointed heels. She was screaming something about her new sofa. I regained a fuller reality and realized what had happened. When I went out my cigarette took a different course, rolling out of my fingers and down the side of her wine-colored velvet sofa. The place was a mess. The sofa was charred, as were both end tables. I'd burned down half the poor peculiar girl's fucking loft, for God's sake. She had managed her own bucket brigade, and everything was soaked in pools of ash and gray water, including me. She obviously didn't think, or care, to remove me before she put out the couch. She was furious. Her hump was visibly gyrating counter-clockwise. I wasn't going to stand still for any more of this bullshit. She had already insulted me by hinting, not once but twice, that I needed a bath. I slid toward the door, jacket in hand. When she turned her back, trying to salvage something from the drawer of a steaming file cabinet, I opened the door, hopped the staircase, and speared straight down. That's the type of thing that would happen to Iggy, I thought.

MISDEEDS IN THE PROJECTION BOOTH

This managerial position at AWT-BAG is beginning to expose its own shortcomings (so to speak). Today, for the third day in a row, I was besieged by a mob of hostile nellies midway through the feature because no one was making the reel changes up in the projection booth, leaving the screen blank and silent for annoying stretches of time. I knew what the problem was and assured the savage throng that the error would be corrected posthaste, utilizing my tight jeans' undulating motions to temporarily stun and mesmerize them, then taking the old domination route and barking out my demand that they return to their seats and shut up while I took command of the situation.

I went upstairs to the projection booth and changed the reel myself, satisfying the masses and gathering a slight round of applause for my authority in crisis. Now I was left to deal with the other problem, which was at that very moment howling from prolonged ejaculation behind the door to my right. You see, my usual projectionist is none other than the infamous Warhol superstar himself, Tiny Tommy Salmonella, but he's away shooting some Spaghetti Western, and has been replaced for the last two weeks by his younger brother. He's been making a nice piece of change for himself by taking the wealthy swells of our clientele into a small sofa-filled room aside the projection booth and packing their fudge for prices only the kin of a true superstar can demand. I admire this enterprise, not to mention the true worthiness of his performance—he's got the same uptown types coming back daily, utilizing a waiting list. But while he's in there doing his four-legged-monster-in-love-with-the-strange routine, I'm left running up here every ten minutes, changing reels in the wrong sequence and doing this Amazon dance with yards of monster celluloid which surround the room like killer vines closing in. Yesterday they attacked my ankle like boa constrictors covered with scales of tiny naked blonde boys. Something must be done. I may have to send some novitiate up to the cloistered abbey and inform the abbot himself about his protégé's misdeeds. Either that or have Tommy's brother cut me in for a piece, so to speak.

A SITUATION WORSENS

I'm beginning to have second thoughts regarding the validity of Gloria's theory that I can overcome my heroin addiction by the simple process of shooting up vast quantities of speed with her twenty times daily . . . not to mention the oral ingestion of ever-increasing quantities of barbiturates toward each midnight. I've never had that lifeguard look, but when I ran into D.M.Z. today, he mentioned that my normal iridescent paleness is gradually taking on a greenish tint . . . "It's a bit like one of those radium-laced bulbs that hang on a string from the light fixture in the bathroom; you know, they sort of glow in the dark."

I suggested he might do a portrait, but he doubted he could find or even mix any such color. "Maybe in a month or so; I've got an extra gallon of evergreen I just used to paint the kitchen up at Samantha's." What a guy. I love that wacky sense of humor.

"You should have passed on the plastic arts," I yelled as he departed across Union Square. "You could have made it big as a comic on the Borscht-Belt circuit. And you wouldn't have had to change your name, either."

Seriously, something has got to be done about this situation. Tomorrow I start to consider variations on this theme. I don't know how much longer I can hold my sanity above sea level with my life these days nothing but one long, unyielding comic interlude.

MEETING ANDREA

I walked into the back room of Max's tonight, a little more loaded than I had thought I was when I left the house. I was holding my hand up into the laser beam, letting the light pass through and considering the possibility that I had, perhaps, missed the vein on the last shot, and thus the rush was just coming on, slowly and with a vengeance. Lost in this rumination, hand still poised in the beam passing red through my palm and onto the white wall, where it simply hung like a stigmata, Andrea comes up to me and leans into my ear, "Wouldn't it be nice if we could pass through the light, instead of the opposite, such as you are now experiencing?" That's quite a non sequitur, I thought to myself, not thinking Andrea had it in her. She is the newest of Andy's stable of whacked-out superstars, a Jewish princess from Queens who has adopted the name of her mentor, i.e., Andrea Warhol. I looked down at her; she was only about four-foot-ten. "Then we would have to move at the speed of light, and the first rule of the law of relativity is that, although one can move at 99.9 percent of that speed, it is impossible to equal the speed itself, since that is the point of relativity itself." I was quite pleased with myself for spitting this out with such alacrity, as ripped-out-of-my-brain as I was, and slyly peered around, hoping someone at a nearby table had picked up on the drift and was as impressed as I was with myself. Nothing happening there—they were all busy impressing someone else themselves. The real world is hard on the ego and the back room of Max's is out of the question altogether.

"I know a faster speed," Andrea spoke up. I had forgotten about her, although she was amazingly sexy, with a body that would fit balanced in your hands like a boxed edition of Proust.

"What would that be?" I asked. I was switching gears . . . forget about being a conceited asshole . . . I was now trying to get over on her.

"The speed of death," she replied. I had a stupid smile on my face, which I lost clumsily on hearing her answer.

"Huh?"

"You know, you hear about these people who have accidents and their heart stops beating for a time and they're pronounced clinically dead. Then some hot-shit doctor runs in and revives them. It's like . . . those people always describe the same sensation . . . of entering a long tunnel and passing into the purest light, and becoming almost one with that light . . . and just then they're brought back . . . but they *did* really pass through that light, and would have become the light itself if the doctor didn't fuck things up, that is."

"How would you like to continue this later, come home with me, I mean . . . ?" I was realizing as I said this that I was seriously stoned, as seriously as one could get without being unconscious under a toilet sink somewhere strange.

"Not tonight," she went on, as if she didn't even hear what I had said, but knew I was going to say it because everybody did, sooner or later, every night of her life, "Why don't you come see me tomorrow night . . . I live right on Park South, right up the street, about eight . . . no, five-to-eight . . . p.m., natch. You'll see something special."

"I will certainly be there." I needed to sit, or fall.

"You're Catholic?"

"I was," I stumbled, "but I'm on hiatus."

"Don't kid around about such things. You're not as smart as you think . . . none of these fuckers are." She raised her voice, pointing around the room, "That's another rule of relativity."

I was impressed by that . . . almost as impressed as by the way she looked walking away.

MEETING ANDREA AGAIN

In the two weeks I've been here, the apartment that Gloria got me for this summer has turned into one vast closet. If I let go of my tendency toward excessive neatness for a single day, things just get messier and messier. So I'm frantically overturning piles of clothing, trying to find something worthy of a subtle pose as I enter Andrea's place tonight for our coming hours of good times, lust, defiance, high hi-jinx, sex-approaching-a-new-decade. Sweetness and possibilities unparalleled. And I'm late and . . . shit, the only thing reasonably unfilthy is this semi-fucking cowboy shirt. I'll have to go with it, in lieu of smelling like Lou Bova— a guy I grew up with whose "body language" had a one-word vocabulary. I might be in luck. She may have a fetish. When your wardrobe consists of nothing but a phony cowboy shirt and denims, you have to hope for fixations.

I inject and speed out the door. It's another one of those steel-blue nights on Park Avenue South, and the laser I have grown obsessed with is sharp as a beacon. It's menacing looking, as if someone drilled a hole in the side of a canister of plutonium and it spit out this seriously harmful light. I want to stick my hand in its path like I do in the back room of Max's, where its intricate journey ends, but it's five flights up and beyond my reach. The higher it gets the more it obsesses me. I notice it passes right by the address which Andrea gave me. And now, looking down on pavement level for the first time since I turned onto the street, I notice something else. It's not reassuring. I stab my pockets for the vial of Valium . . . frayed edges . . . *nauseum incipius*.

The red twirling lights of five police cars and an ambulance are clashing into each other and bouncing off the hoods of passing cars, carrying the whole mess right up the block to me. I break into a dead run. I know without looking that the building they're in front of is the address she gave me, and I think I know something more—more than I want. I get there . . . oh, God . . . it's her. She's dead. She jumped and she's lying there naked and dead and covered with a blanket that had been leaning a few minutes before against a spare tire in some cop car. She's holding a can of diet cola in one hand and a pair of rosary beads in the other. Her head is smashed on one side. Her hair, her fine, blond hair, is like a tangled net with small shining red fish, trapped and lifeless. I stagger backward onto the hood of a car and hug the hood ornament until I'm almost twisting it off. A cop moves me away. I notice this guy Emilio, a Factory sycophant and quasi-aristocrat-utility-man, heading toward me. I'm about to tell him to piss off, but he gets out enough words to bite. He asks me if I had a date with her and I tell him I did. Then he goes on that he too was supposed to meet her at eight, and he points out seven or nine other Max's habitués who are hovering around and explains that she had made dates with all of them for the same time.

"I guess she wanted an audience, you know?"

"No, I wouldn't know. Why don't you not continue with what you're saying and just tell me if anyone saw her jump."

"I saw her," he replied, breaking his English with finesse. "I always arrive early. It was strange, you know?"

"No, I don't. What do you mean?"

"It was like she was jumping onto the laser beam . . . as if she were trying to grab it . . . but with her mouth, not her hands. Like she wanted to swallow it."

"Or be swallowed by it," I mumbled, remembering her talk last night.

"What?"

"Never mind . . . You mean she passed right through the beam as she fell?"

"Yes . . . and, well, it was really very strange. I know I was in shock and all, seeing this but, she yelled out something very strange before she jumped. I don't know what, but I was in a state, very strange. You see, it seemed from down here like some illusion of optics, yes? It seemed that for a moment, like a whole second of time, that she actually hung onto the beam from the laser as if it were a line for clothes. And the can of soda and the rosary? She was a Jew, no?"

I walked away, without any acknowledgment to Emilio, though I was in debt to him for what he had said. She *was* a Jew. And last night she asked me, her last words, I believe, if I were Catholic. Why did she ask me to come five minutes before the others? I imagine that she thought I was such an asshole, with my absolute and overwhelming love of my own bullshit rap, that she wanted to show me, before the others got there, something about a genuine absolute—*the* absolute in action. I could talk all night about relativity and the speed of light, but she was going to *prove* her point, in complete and enduring terms, about her notion—that crazed, yet beautiful, phrase, "the speed of death." And why did she decide to jump before I or the rest of the boys (aside from the punctually-at-ease Emilio) had arrived? Was it charity for me . . . sparing me the sight? More likely it was just disregard. Why should she think of me at all in the face of her trip into the passing of light? Why did she ask me at all? A laugh? I'm laughing so hard it's becoming very difficult to breathe. I go home and stare in the big mirror. I see too much of myself there.

LIMBO

I duck into a strange church to rest, absorb some silence. Sit beneath that station of the cross where Christ's face is washed clean by a woman's veil. I read in the *Times* last week that an ecclesiastical council has taken the official position that the Church has, in fact, *never had* an official position concerning the state of "Limbo," that in-between place for children who die without receiving the grace of Baptism. Pascal died young because of such statements, but he died laughing.

I think the Church is way off on this. I know such a place exists . . . I feel the seeds which have dropped from that plane explode softly, like gun barrels in a silent movie, inside my belly.

Didn't you ever want to starve all the flesh from your body, down to the pure bone? Don't you want to take a sledgehammer and pulverize those bones to a sheer, white powder, and throw it into the air . . . just to see which way the wind is blowing?

ENDING THE SPELL

Two days have passed since I ended my methedrine-seconal alliance with Gloria. I believe it was a Polaroid picture that caused the final decision. It was a typical shot among many this past summer; I was naked, early morning, just awake, the streets seventeen flights below being ravaged by machines run on compressed air that seemed to be emanating directly from my brain. She took the picture as I lay in bed. "You look like a Modigliani," she said in that breathless burst which indicated she had already taken care of *that* business. "I feel like shit with bad teeth," I muttered, taking in hand the Polaroid print she flipped beside me and watching it slowly surface over sixty seconds with a sober scrutiny that made it suddenly unique. In that literal minute, all these strange emotions unclogged like fat-laden main arteries and rushed to my vision. The sun, split into shafts by the blinds, seemed clean and sympathetic. It was radiant in the photo, which was just beginning to reveal lines on a background green like government paint. I took a quick glance around the room. There was a sense of *jamais vu*. What had always seemed like the mindless gaze of some genius doll suddenly seemed like the fearful eyes of a child on a ledge suffering from vertigo.

Then the features of my naked body began to appear. It seemed to take longer than usual for the picture to reach a finished clarity, as if its subject's pulse had barely existed.

I could hardly stand to look. The ribs stuck out like the inner shell of a toy boat. The cheeks were sunken deep enough to hide pins within the crevices. The eyes had the look of a pathologist's wet dream. I was not going to allow that person to continue as me any longer. I got up out of the bed and dressed in a single motion. I swear if Gloria had tried in any way to stop me . . . if she had even spoken a word as I pushed my way out that door, I would have taken her neck in my hands and squeezed the photo right into it.

BIRD OF PREY

I've put three more days now between myself and the cycle of speed and downers I've been running on with Gloria for the past summer. That makes five days since the last violation of my rapidly retreating veins. It's not as if I'm some prisoner in a cartoon marking off the days in chalk lines on the wall, which would be most unseemly against the frescoed walls of my borrowed apartment, but it does feel good to have broken that circle of artificial energy abetted by artificial sleep. There certainly exists a difference between my sleep, then and now. In fact, I spent the first two days indulging in the genuine article. I could witness in my dreams the last efforts of the remaining speed. It was like walking a long, bitter avenue of frenzied happenings which, over each passing hour, grew calmer and focused as the residue of drugs drained out of my system. The spirals of noise, harsh and diffused, eventually settled into the delight of dream's true dialogue. The characters passing through lost their beastly sneers; they slowly took on a nobility. They gestured easily with their hands. At last the dreams, lovely or nightmarish, have slowed to their own natural rhythm.

And my senses, after a few days of impartial lethargy (it felt, as I moved through the streets one afternoon, that I was not walking but being carried, eyes half shut, on the

back of an ox or donkey), have returned, intact and height-
ened. That's no mystery; there is always a kind of inverse
high after the initial withdrawal from any drug used over
time. Yesterday, watching a cockroach make the fatal error
of hopping from the kitchen counter onto the griddle heating at full flame on the stove, I could swear I heard this
high-pitched whine of anguish. And today as I was de-
frosting the refrigerator (while I'm still wallowing in the
joys of the commonplace), I found myself realizing that
the sound of the ice cracking apart on the roof of the
freezer bore an uncanny similarity to that of the wings of
a trained bird of prey. I imagined a falcon flapping in place,
talons still planted on the owner's leather-bound wrist. The
sound grew louder as it melted over time. I shut my eyes
and watched dozens of yellow-and-black-winged birds, some
with arrowhead markings on their straining chests, with
dangerous eyes like cyanide capsules, flying continuously
from my refrigerator and circling the room, disappearing
(or returning back into the machine?), where the final layer
had melted into a puddle the size of the kitchen, so deep
the linoleum was beginning to curl at its edges. Sensual
splendor can leave one horrible mess, but God, that was
lovely.

TINY TORTURES

Poetry readings just don't cut it for me the way they used
to. There are only a handful of poets who truly know *how*
to read their work, who can take the audience *out there*. I've
been a regular at the readings at St. Mark's Church, down
on 10th Street, since I was sixteen, and it's astonishing how
boring some of the really great poets are when they ascend
that podium. I've heard an anthology of my favorite poems,
so alive when I read them on the page, butchered en route
from the poet's mouth. You can almost see the words dropping in front of the podium onto the liturgical red carpet,
squirming in circles like fumigated bugs, before even

reaching the audience. One night, when one of my favorite writers was hacking to bits a short story in a severe mon-otone, I nodded out and saw his book wrenched out of his hands by some invisible force of wrath and justice, which lifted it up and nailed it to the huge wooden cross behind the reader.

My enjoyment, or lack of it, is academic at this point, however. The fact is, I work here now. I'm Anne Waldman the boss lady's "assistant." That means I must fold chairs before and after the readings, and hold the contribution basket in people's faces at the intermission and the end (and I can honestly say I've only skimmed off the donations on nights when my dealer, or anybody's dealer, was in the audience—or at home). I also have to bounce the noisy winos who wander in, or the occasional heckler. So I'm pretty much held captive, a prisoner of mumblings, poor phrasing, elision and the caustic whinings of our "guests" every Wednesday night, week after week.

But of course, there are wonderful exceptions, and often it is some poet whose writings you never really got into while reading his or her books by your lonesome. Then they step up and suddenly you are riveted, it all falls into place and you can't wait to get home and reread their entire output.

Lately, they've also been inviting these "performance artists" to do their acts. This is just another name for the same folks who did "Happenings" in the sixties. By the very definition, these performance artists should have a way with an audience. I mean, it's clear by the nature of the medium that their art just don't exist without a crowd. Some of them are ingenious, enlightening and entertaining as well. Some of them are quite funny actually, though often that is not their intention. Then again, many of them are wrapped in so many layers of pretense that it would be a performance piece in itself to strip them all away. They are boundless in their energy to bore, and they are so smug you want to go after their most sensitive bodily parts with rusty tweezers. Well, it's no different from the poets: when it's good, it's great . . . when it's bad, it's wretched. The former you take home; the latter you leave behind, feet up on that red carpet, or nailed to the cross-beams.

Actually, I shouldn't knock the genre since I myself was a performance artist once . . . for a day. I was about seventeen, and the event called for about twenty painters, musicians and poets to each do a "piece" no longer than three minutes. I remember it was on a Sunday afternoon because I woke up at my friend's apartment, which we referred to as "Headquarters," the morning of the show, on my knees and hugging the porcelain in the bathroom with a cough syrup and beer hangover and absolutely no idea what to do for my three minutes in the spotlight of Art. I had already dismissed the idea of boiling a three-minute egg . . . it just didn't seem to have the necessary *edge*. Then, right there in the john, washing the puke from my chin at the bathtub faucet, I saw the answer: a hearty-sized cockroach, trying in vain to scale the slick sides of the tub. I dashed into the living room and grabbed a small brown paper bag from among the debris of empty beer bottles and sleeping bodies, then returned and scooped in the insect, shaking him securely into the bottom of the bag, cautiously folding it on top. I had half of my routine, and in the cabinet beneath the kitchen sink I found the other half, which I threw into a knapsack along with the bagged bug. I waited for the others to wake, we smoked some grass and watched the usual Sunday morning cartoons. I split around an hour before the four P.M. showtime.

I arrived at the gig, which was at a large ground-floor space across from Max's Kansas City, right as things were beginning. The woman who organized things came over and told me when I'd go on, which turned out to be, for-tunately, toward the end. She asked me if I had a title for my "event," but I couldn't think of anything off-hand. I told her no, I didn't have a name for it. "I'll just introduce you and call your piece 'Untitled.'" Well . . . okay.

Things moved along quickly, the woman in charge introducing each performer and title over the microphone. The place was packed, and since there was no one stage where the pieces were performed, the crowd just moved from one end of the room to the other, gathering around the spot where the action took place. Some of the events were clever, others made the allotted three minutes seem endless. There was a musician who subjected everyone to this viciously high-pitched tone at a decibel level that had people clapping hands over their ears, grinding their teeth in agony. Some had to duck out onto Park Avenue South. I could even feel my roach banging against the walls of his bag, freaked out by the sound. After that, an art critic and mediocre poet covered the windows of the place with long strips of black tape, forming x's. Some pompous geek behind me was hailing the wonderful statement it made. "It has a lovely negative capability," he informed his girlfriend. I began laughing so hard people surrounded me, thinking I was doing my performance.

Then a woman painter did a three-minute striptease. The stragglers outside on the sidewalk scurried back in for that one. When she shimmied off her dress the only thing she wore beneath it was a huge alarm clock on a belt. It sounded off right at the end of three minutes. I liked that one.

I kept checking out my roach to see if he (or she . . . though I think it was a *bull* roach) was doing alright. It seemed to be holding up. The organizer came over and told me I was on after the next person. I wandered over to a corner to gather myself together. I was suddenly not only nervous, but depressed. To me, the piece was already done, at the moment the concept first came (actually, crawled) to me in the bathroom at Headquarters. I didn't see the point in doing it now in front of all these people. I was satisfied with the way it went down in my head, all the rest was just ego, all the rest was just, as the man said, the madness of *Art*.

But I realized I was just playing head games, justifying an escape because of my stage fright. My theory was no more than an inverted elitism. If I'm not gonna shut up, I've gotta put up. And it was about that time.

I ran over to the organizer, who was at the microphone, about to announce me. I whispered into her ear that I had changed my mind, that I did have a title for my piece. She stepped back to the mike and it sounded over the crowd: "Here is Jim Carroll, performing his work, 'Tiny Tortures.'"

I moved to the center of the room, then signaled the people to close in as tight as possible around me to see, reserving only enough room for me to operate. I knelt down in the middle of the circle they had formed and reached into the knapsack placed at my side. I pulled out the paper bag with one hand, then, with the other, a can of Raid. I undid, slowly, the neat folds on top of the bag, then turned it over and gently shook it.

The roach landed on his back upon the highly varnished wooden floor. He didn't move. I felt lumps in my throat, lungs, heart and bowels. If the little fucker had croaked on me I was up shit's creek. Then to my great relief he flipped over and spun around, as if the whole thing had been purposefully done for dramatic effect. I quickly raised up the can of deadly spray, and not a moment too soon. He was making a dash for it . . . right toward the sea of dilettante shoes. I cocked the trigger to the can and blasted him in one long barrage. He turned and headed in the other direction, but I laid down a well-timed strategic pattern of quick bursts. He was hit and hit bad, again and again . . . but he struggled on. Dazed by the malodorous insecticide, he began to move in circles, rallied by the applause of the crowd, whose mood and gestures had suddenly shifted from that of hip supporters of the arts into crazed rednecks in the heat of a cockfight. I kept up my spurts . . . pools of the stuff were forming. What an adversary, what a genuine trooper I had picked from the tub that morning!

But, in the end, no matter how much heart, the roach could not stand up against the savage forces of Art, not to mention Raid. It finally crumbled in its tiny tracks, its legs sort of just spreading out to the sides. The incredible part is it held on to just under the three-minute mark before collapsing. Of course I felt compassion for the little vermin, but as far as the event went, things couldn't have gone better. The audience loved it.

The following week, in both *The East Village Other* and *The Village Voice,* I was singled out as a stone rave in their reviews of the show. One referred to the "keen, trenchant commentary which the piece made on urban decay." The other called it "a non-verbal demonstration on the horrors of Vietnam."

I agree. All that was exactly what flashed through my mind as I bagged the insect in Headquarters' bathroom that morning. And, I might add, there was a large dose of *negative capability* as well. It just goes to show you how random are our gains in the Performance (a.k.a. Conceptual) Art trade. Fact is, the only point I was making is the point you get . . . then as now.

BIGGER THAN MOST

I have been taking part in the weekly Friday-night poker games. It's all painters and poets and we play at the studio of a photorealist on Saint Mark's Place. I'm a pretty cautious player. I never lose big; I never win much either. All in all, this last month I've come out on the down end of under ten dollars. I just don't have the concentration, I guess. I pay more attention to the small-chat. You never know what vampires some of your peers are until you pass them a fresh deck. For my part, the only time I've ever seen the

killer instinct emerge from myself was the last time I got
hit in the head with a rock. I went wild for the guy's ear . . . bit
a quarter-inch off the upper lobe. When these things happen I have to take the guy out fast; within the first thirty
seconds I puke and exhaust myself to incapacity. My
adrenaline causes serious disarray in my thought process . . . i.e., the guy who winged me was Italian, and I came
at him screaming, "I will kill you, you dirty fucking Jew."
It's a disturbing scenario. I suppose that's why I enjoy these
card games; I'm too mediocre to grow incensed. It's a pleasure to bide your time outside any chance at brilliance.

But some of your friends grow strange; they take it right
into your face. I smoked some grass before the game last
night and had to drop out. Things got frightening. Faces
distorted; fingers ran along the edge of the cards as if they
were casually sharpening a blade. Besides, I discovered
from the first few hands that it is not financially healthy to
play on smoke. It's time to quit when queens start to wink
and dance the "hitchhiker"; when you get a hard-on being
dealt the nine of spades . . . when the jack of hearts begins
to drip red, evoking the mysteries of the Eucharist. I folded
my cards and losses, laid out a plate of antipasto and played
the harpsichord down the far end. I was feeling like young
Wolfie M. until someone yelled from the table, "Will you
please bag that fucking wop piano; that's the worst shit I
ever heard." You just know that man was losing big.

But tonight . . . tonight I was in my element. We walked
into Julian's on 14th to shoot some nine ball. There was
Ted, another poet, a painter who always wins big at the
poker games and myself. Pool is the other side of the coin
for me. I was once good enough at it to feel free to terrorize
myself and everyone around me when I fucked up. Last
week I put a dent in some spinner's bee-hive hairdo when
I blew a hanger and javelined the cue stick toward the
window. Her old man poured me out in the rain. I had to
therefore enter with caution tonight, sneakers tied and set
to flee. The exhaust of my temper tends to seriously pollute

my life and its freedom of choice. But the guy wasn't there, and a different man was behind the cash register. It wasn't the one who had banned me for eternity.

So we lag for partners. It turns out Ted and I will team up against the other two. I want to play the nine ball for five dollars, but we decide on a fucking ace. This is unfair. I don't bitch about these guys raising me without limit at cards . . . why spite me my edge at pool? I spent a lot of time on my game when I was young in order to exploit this edge . . . more time and energy than, say, they spent in order to wear a straight face while they are bluffing a friend out of his pants. (Shit, when I try to bluff I look the other guy in the eyes and laugh hysterically. It tends to ruin the effect.) Well, the money doesn't matter. None of us can really afford to lose. But I do want that nine ball for my own, and I want to pocket it with finesse. And that's the way it turns out. After five games Ted and I are up on them by the same number of dollars. And what do they do? They wimp out and quit. Can you imagine? They must have won eighty dollars between them last night at poker (and spent considerable time letting us be reminded of the fact on the way over here), and they walk after being shot down for a measly five bills. This is small. This is truly a revelation. You forget, in the force of admiring some people's talent, that artists can be assholes too, and bigger than most.

DYLAN AND THE KGB

I went uptown to Town Hall tonight to catch a reading by the Russian poet Voznesensky. I've never really gotten into his work, but it's certainly got an edge which his fellow countryman, Yevtushenko, couldn't touch without drawing blood. As Frank O'Hara said, "He couldn't carry the hat worn by Mayakovsky's horse," and for me his poem "Babi Yar," has always been a yawn as wide as that rotting trench itself. But Anne Waldman tells me Voznesensky is worth another shot, and since she's got the tickets, the price seems right.

Having laid this enthusiastic riff on me, however, Anne greets me at her place with the news that she can't make it. She tells me I should go anyway . . . Ginsberg, Peter O., Ed Sanders and "some other couple," will meet me there in the adjoining seats. I hop on the train. Why shouldn't I? If it does get unbearable, I can always hop over to Times Square and play insect anonymous.

I arrive through the mosque-like, tiled doorways of the hall, take the mezzanine stairway, and find myself doing William Powell's "Thin Man" bit when an elderly matron snatches my ticket and says, "Walk this way." So I imitate her walk as she leads me to the front row of the mezzanine, amusing only myself, because I am looked on most queerly by the seated, poetic suits around me. I greet Allen and Ed and Peter and the aforementioned "couple," which, it turns out, consists of no less than Mr. Bob (call me Bob) Dylan and his wife Sara, the sad-eyed lady of the lowlands herself. Sara bends some knees in an elegant dip, too far down the aisle for contact. Dylan, whose hand is close enough to shake, twists his mouth into a cipher and mumbles a tangy, "How yer doin,' " leaving my hand hanging somewhere between either end of Ed Sanders' moustache. I'm pulling some curly barbs from Ed's face out of my finger-nails as the houselights begin to dim. My timing was as perfect as the air Dylan left on my hand.

The reading seemed fine as far as Voz's Russian ren-derings went. They had a steady passion, without the rav-ing, motherland histrionics of Yevtushenko (whom I refuse to mention again, as I am getting tired typing out his name, having to check the spelling each time). Voz's work did a sort of relaxed backstroke to your heart. I enjoyed it, and he timed it just right . . . left himself with breath to spare on the shore. Too many poets go and swim out too far during their readings to ever make it back at all, never mind with any degree of grace left for the final, critical strokes. The translations, however, care of some CCNY literature professor with eyes like tiny waffle irons, were just horrendous. Voz himself seemed to politely cringe from his stage-bound chair. It was obvious he wanted to pace, preferably along a bar rail. It was clearly time to check out Dylan.

He wasn't giving much away. Actually, I don't think anyone around us knew who he was. All eyes were on Allen, sitting up with the straight, Zen posture of a man who knows how to take a really proper shit. Dylan was sunk low in his red-velvet seat, expensive tasty threads hanging well on his post-motorcycle crack-up slump. His eyes had this atavistic quality. "Yes, I know all about it . . ." I thought, "but can he *spell?*" Finally, he turned my way and eyes met . . . they glittered with an outlandish charm, not at all unsexy, and his pupils seemed to reach out and shake mine, a pact to the synch of our boredom. Allen whispered something about the reader's "timidity," but the professor was just then closing up shop. He never even made it into the water.

Houselights rising, we got up and seemed to stretch in unison, except for Allen, who was literally hopping up the stairs in anticipation of greeting Voz. (I was later told that it was mainly through Ginsberg's efforts, lobbying at the Russian Consulate and making calls to the U.S. State Department, who must have been thrilled to do him a favor, that Voz was vouchsafed permission to make the tour . . . considered as he was by his own government something of an "unsafe factor" outside the USSR, especially in countries where leather jackets are available off the rack.) We followed Allen's lead to the stage, where Voz, the poet W. H. Auden, who made the introductions before I had arrived, the unbearable professor, and a shadowy person with Slavic features, who seemed by his grimace to be desperately attempting to effect an astral projection on the spot, were all huddled about talking. I was intermittently checking out Dylan through the trip downstairs, and through

the crowd. He had a slumping, camouflaged way of moving, like an aged and wise chameleon, perfected by years
of ducking out of joints inconspicuously. Nobody recog-
nized him whatsoever . . . it made me want to rush over
and slap my arm around him in embrace, yelling, "Hey,
wake up, this is fucking Bob Dylan, for God's sake . . . what's
the matter with you people? . . . I will kill you all immediately and fast." But I knew Bob wouldn't want that, and
I'm the type to appreciate another man's wishes. I simply
followed him and his wife, who really was quite lovely,
through the stage door.

She was melancholy too, this Sara . . . hell, she was flat-
out sad-looking, cradling some deep frustration of rage in
her eyes with the casual cover of one who had made it all
portable long ago. And she was dressed to the
nines . . . strictly Bergdorf's and Tiffany . . . if she had any
of that gypsy blood which he often sang of, it had been
purged long ago in the confines of some clinic in Zurich.
This was a woman who, gone shopping, would bring back
a hell of a lot more than a lousy pair of boots of Spanish
leather. I admired her; she had the bearing and moves
which very few could have maintained for long in the force
of the man she had married. She also had some gears all
her own, slowly and secretly clicking in the deep, deep
recesses. And, right this moment, she was shaking the hand
of W. H. Auden.

I was next to shake the great poet's hand, thinking no
one else on this stage even comes close, and that old cur-
mudgeon knows it, too. I was surprised when he remembered me from our previous encounter, when Edwin Denby
introduced us in the B&H Dairy Restaurant right off Saint
Mark's Place, where Auden lives. He even made reference
to a poem of mine in a rather old issue of *Poetry* magazine.
That little bit of poet-to-poet patter certainly gave me the
cockiness to greet Voznesensky on my own terms. He had
a firm, Stavrogin-like handshake, however, that nearly buc-

kled my knees and elicited a small whimper from my humbled self, leaving me only to mumble, "Wonderful . . . simply wonderful," over and over until somebody shoved me out of the way. I wound up on the perimeter of a conversation between Ginsberg and Auden. Auden was querying Allen (so to speak) regarding a recent group reading they had both apparently taken part in. He wanted to know if Allen was still playing "that silly, little squeeze-box thing," and chanting those "dreadful, quasi-Hindu" mantras, which had, it seems, driven Auden out of the building at their last encounter. I thought Allen would set some fur flying but he softly deferred, and the conversation escalated into a rather serious discussion on Hinduism, Christopher Isherwood, and readings in general. Needless to say, I remained safely on the outskirts. I figured I had plenty more time to pick up, before I began making my deliveries.

After Auden and his small entourage leave, we find ourselves surfacing onto the street and throwing out suggestions about where to take Voz for a bite of some capitalist chow. A single voice neatly projects over the street noise: "How about the Kettle of Fish?" The nasal whine makes it unnecessary to turn, but we all do. It's Dylan delivering his only line thus far, and if it isn't a good choice, nobody is about to contradict it . . . in fact, if he had said, "How about us all going to the S&M fag bars down near the docks, entering the men's room and licking the barnacles from the toilets dry," everyone would have chorused back, "Hey, swell idea . . . that's a notion, Bobby." So we grab two cabs and make it down Bleecker. I notice that the mysterious, Slavic-featured fellow is joining us, insistently riding alongside Voz in the cab. He has already been identified, in passing, as the poet's "translator," but his English, from what I've been able to suss out thus far, is fairly awful. I don't think there is really much question in any of our minds about which branch of the Soviet government he in fact represents, but no one is broaching the subject. Anyway, as we arrive at the restaurant, he reaches deep for some local currency and takes care of the meter, leaving the driver stiff. I drop a buck on the seat beside the driver and enter the restaurant.

Since I got in last, I figure there's no way I'm about to get into the same booth as Dylan and Ginsberg and Voz. It turns out I'm right about that. In fact, I wind up being frozen out of the booth scene altogether, and get laid down like a bread basket at a table for two with the translator, of all people, as my companion.

It wasn't that bad. I took the opportunity to bombard him with questions, asking mainly about the extent of the drug situation back in the U.S.S.R. He denied the existence of any such situation, informing me the country was, "Free (sic) as a hound's tooth."

"That's *clean* as a . . ." I began.

"Yes, yes . . . whatever," he interrupted, obviously much sharper at our language than he seemed.

"Well, this friend of mine was visiting Russia," I went on, "and he told me he ran into these folks who said they were art students, and who took him to a party and offered him some grass . . . uh, marijuana."

"Your friend, I think, is fooling you, perhaps?"

"No, I don't think so. Anyway, he said the shit was garbage . . . Christmas-tree smoke."

"Christmas trees?" he burst forward, ready to secure another vice of the West, "They smoke Christmas trees?"

"No, no," I spoke quickly, "This is only an expression to describe weak marijuana . . . my friend said your country, in effect, has *beat* dope."

"No dope in Soviet Union . . . I tell you this."

"Yeah, *big* dope in Soviet Union," I replied, voice flaring, "*big* dope in America, too . . . I tell *you* this . . . and *das vedanya*, you goon-spy-KGB-mo-fo!" I pushed back the table and bolted up, shuffled across the sawdust floor and out the door. I didn't even say goodnight to Bob. Bob Dylan.

CENTRAL PARK, LATE FALL

Ted Berrigan and I, after spending the morning at a screening of *The General* at the Museum of Modern Art, took to the park to catch the late fall colors before they shook themselves loose from the limbs and disappeared damply beneath chic boots and winter.

After a perfunctory scan of the zoo, we crossed the Sheep Meadow. There was nobody else in sight; it made the meadow seem twice as vast. "I feel like some refugee," Ted cracked. I picked up from there and spoke in a wavering accent, "Yes comrade, we are a long way from Moscow, but soon we shall reach the village of Peroshki, and my good cousin Lubrigosh will give us work bundling his wheat harvest." Ted carried on without missing a beat, "Yes, he is a good man; you have told me about his wife's soup."

We were midway through the huge field now, just passing out of the shadows cast by the block of three-and-a-half-star hotels lining Central Park South. The early winter sun offered no real warmth, but it did provide a placebo effect. We loosened our coats; Ted was wearing the green one with the hood that I lent him last year, which he had no intention of giving back. He said it made him feel like he "was always on his way to the big game."

The trees we were approaching on the far side blazed with color. A brighter orange snaked through the deep mauve, forming strange glyphs and symbols, like brands burnt into the hide of some Druid beasts. They were as enchanting as anything the museum had to offer. They also possessed that deceptive quality of great art. As we moved closer, the splendor yielded by distance was stripped away, and we saw how the November wind and chill had taken its toll. What had seemed full and overwhelming only two minutes and three hundred yards earlier, now seemed barren and strained. The tight, discarded leaves were crackling in piles, ankle high, beneath us. We realized all that was left to the branches was a determined outline of dogged, stray remains; just enough, combined with distance, to provide a ghostly image of its former self. Nature has a way with illusion that even the greatest art cannot match. The fire-branded monster seen from mid-meadow was now no more than a scrawny tree.

As we headed for Cleopatra's Needle, we turned up for one last look. We were too close to catch the magic. There was just a lone squirrel, laid back on his haunches, staring down at us. He made a triumphant clicking sound and raised his head gracefully, an attitude of majesty, as if he were responsible for the stunning work of forgery to which we had fallen victim.

THE BELLS

There was a benefit for Timothy Leary tonight at the Café à Go Go in the Village . . . poets, musicians, theater people, all giving their time to raise legal fees for one of the man's many misunderstandings with the law. They asked me to read, but I said, "later." There has always been something mildly abhorrent about that guy. It has a lot to do with that condescending, salacious smile, just like an advertising executive leering over some bunny at the Playboy Club. He's always seemed to put so much energy into contempt, fueled by a spite that is positively radiant.

So I'm not giving him any time at the podium, but I do go along with Anne and Ted to check things out. The list of performers is fairly luminous, but things are pretty subdued. The crowd is rubbernecking for celebrities and chattering away, not paying too much attention to the staged goings-on. This is one of those functions with a fifty-fifty mixture of uptown dilettantes in beaded gowns and black tie, and the slagheap from beneath 14th Street. It's comical actually, the way the two groups mingle for a certain time designated by some odd sense of etiquette, and then, in a moment, seek their own kind out frantically, as if a bell had struck. Afterwards, it's as if there was a glass partition between the two groups: champagne poured on one side by waiters in snappy suits, and on the other side, paper cups filled with punch of cheap upstate white wine and antifreeze. Any minute, you expect the truck to back in and see bales of hay tossed down on the dirtbag side.

Leary gets up and makes a speech. He's looking good . . . maybe if they have three more benefits like this, he'll be able to buy another suit like the one he's wearing. "*He's* the one responsible for all those bummers you've had," Ted bursts out in a mock cry, "Now's your chance . . . string him up . . . You get the rope, I'll get the tree." This is all in jest, naturally, though some of the folks on the Uptown side take umbrage. They puff up like swamp adders and shake the sequins on their breasts, aghast.

Allen Ginsberg reads a truly lovely poem written on acid, "Wales Visitation." Even the uptowners, still seething with umbrage, listen intently. I don't know where Ginsberg goes when he reads, but he takes you with him.

Then, a surprise to make my evening. Onto the stage, grinning sheepishly as is his way, steps Phil Ochs, guitar in hand. He hasn't performed in a while, and he seems nervous and tentative. I scan the room . . . if these people do not cut the cocktail-chatter scene, I'm not going to silence them with a polite finger to my lips, but with something more in the line of a baseball bat.

Around about my fourteenth year of life, this dude forever changed *it all* for me. As faces sometimes embody the true meaning of words, his face is lined with affection. My legs tighten as my heart tries to push him the final step to the microphone. He complies, hesitantly, then breaks into "The Bells," his version of the Poe poem set to music.

His guitar is blazing, his voice tight at first, but loosening with each word. It's interesting he chose a lyric that he didn't write and, though it's an "up" song, his phrasing is mournful beneath its flawlessness. In the middle of the song I begin to hear a tiny ringing, like one of those bells you put on a cat's collar so it can't sneak up on birds. I move a couple of steps over and see Allen Ginsberg at the bottom of the stage, merrily playing little Tibetan finger-cymbals. Phil is looking down at Allen, throwing him at first something between a scowl and a look of bewilderment, then breaking into a beatific smile. The song ends, and he rushes off the stage.

That was it for Anne and Ted and I, and we left together as we'd arrived, but pumped up from Ochs. It was raining outside, and that seemed as it should. By the time I had reached the top of the stairs leading out of the club, the bottom fell out. I realized how sad that man onstage was. Every gesture he made was that of someone who'd been hit-and-run by time. The result was a partial amnesia . . . a haunting that seemed, to him, deliberate. He knew the accident had happened, but he didn't know when or where, and everything he did, including singing "The Bells" tonight, was part of his search for the answers to that moment, to that time and place.

DR. FEELGOOD

The lining of my jacket is not enough for this vicious winter freeze. It's dawn, and the wind is laughing through the fabric, slashing my unprotected ears. I think for a moment about returning to the apartment and adding on a few layers of clothes and a brim, but I figure it's best to keep moving . . . maybe the Fifth Avenue bus will come along. "It must be the chill off the reservoir in Central Park," some elderly matron wrapped from head to toe in cynical, thick fur says to me out of nowhere as she notices me passing, body parts flung around in spasms. "Must be," I answer, my beet-red face not looking up. "How about letting me stuff those poodles you're walking down my jacket, hee hee . . ." She moves away in small quick steps that crack the thin layers of ice forming on the pavement, saying something that is immediately lifted in a white swirl upward and across the street into the treetops of the park. "That there is what you would call an example of the 'doppler effect,'" speaks a ghost-like voice from a doorman who had taken in the scene right before he disappeared into his radiator-lined alcove. All I know is each winter seems worse, which means we are either at the beginning of a new ice age, or I am turning Puerto Rican.

I make it to the East Side and enter the minuscule foyer of an elegant townhouse through two large doors of brass and teak. There are already four or five people waiting there chattering away, their scented breath visible, rising up and cross-hatching like klieg lights during a movie premiere or bombing attack. One or two of them nod at me, not so much to greet me, but more to assure the others that they have seen me before and I am not about to rob their coats. Within the next five minutes at least a dozen more bodies have crammed in the tiny space, each shivering and each making the same witless comment about the cold. They are a true representation of all types of wealthy New Yorkers. Gucci and Blackglama. The limos are double-parked in a convoy outside. They are all here for one reason, and you know it must be a very good one, because none of them would otherwise tolerate having to stand waiting in such close proximity to another human body, no matter whose prints are hanging on the walls. They are waiting for the doctor. So am I. We are all here, at 5:45 A.M., waiting for Dr. Feelgood.

Dr. Feelgood is, actually, a generic term. There are four of them in New York City, all frequented by the social elite, show business folk, and artists with money. Actually, one of them is not even a doctor, but a dentist; his patients must have the cleanest teeth in town. Of course, none of these people would dare go to any of these quacks if they were the least bit ill. They go for one reason. The reason is the injection. The injection consists of vitamins, specifically B-12, and sundry other elements. These sundry elements vary from one Dr. Feelgood to the other, but basic to each one's formula are calcium, cow's blood, potassium, and the main ingredient, the reason the foyer is full with anxious fur and gray flannel at 5:45 A.M., a whopping dose of pure amphetamine.

This particular physician I am visiting today, Dr. Kroakus, is no doubt the most infamous of all. That's due in large measure to the fact that he happens to be one of his own best patients. Out of the other three, only the dentist, as far as I know, is also on the formula. Though his reputation preceded him by years, I was only introduced to Dr. Kroakus last week by my British patron, an elegant young dude with sharp features, and wavy brown hair halfway down his back. He wears expensive threads, has a fearsome wit, and is accompanied at all times by two outrageously gorgeous women. They are the exact same height, and they couldn't be more than a pound or two apart, weight-wise. They flank him wherever he walks, on each arm like crutches, talking about karma and Bat Masterson.

Immediately after I shook the good doctor's hand he was aiding me in rolling up my sleeve. He drew up the formula, a translucent red in color, out of a vial as a perky nurse tied me off. He had a good touch for a doctor. (They're usually notorious bunglers with a syringe.) The stuff kicked in like a teased mule. It was a strange rush. There was this wave of stinging heat, like a horde of fire ants, that went straight from my balls, right up and out the top of my skull. I found out later that this was the effect of the calcium. It was not at all an unpleasant sensation, and distinctly different from shooting street speed. You felt somehow calmer . . . smooth. I've never been a drinker, but I imagine it's the same difference as good, aged scotch from some rotgut shit. You surely talk as much, but in a lower tone of voice.

That was about two weeks ago, and I've been a regular ever since, arriving each morning a few minutes earlier. The limey patron told the Doc to just chalk up my treatment to his tab, thinking it would give me inspiration to finish off a book of poems. The fact is, I *have* written about

nine or ten new poems since then, which is roughly equal
to the hours I have slept. You might want to check me on
this, but I figure that comes out to something like an hour
and a half per night.

I haven't slept *at all* for the last three days and four
nights. Did I mention that? The thing is that this guy opens
so early (anywhere between 5:15 and 6:00 A.M.) that whenever the inclination to lie down comes over you, say at two
in the morning, you wind up thinking, "Well, heh, I mean,
uh, why bother . . . you know? I mean, the fucker will be
opening within three hours or so, and, uh, besides, you
know, I really kind of *like* those people I run into there . . . I
mean the other early arrivals . . . I have a real sense of
affinity with them." Something like that. It works, too. There's
no one home to contradict me.

So here I am, waiting with a crush of uptown assholes
with who I in fact have absolutely no affinity whatsoever,
and who I hate worse than Richard Nixon. It's so packed
in this vestibule now that I'm sucking fur-balls from the
collar of this dreadful wretch, who keeps insisting to some
gentleman whose eyeballs keep interchanging that it was
"as a matter of record," her daughter that the song "Girl
from Ipanema" was written about. Finally, just as the mob
is beginning to get ugly, the doctor and two nurses arrive
through the doors. A path to the office door opens, the
two sides parting with the snappy precision of some tribal
dance. The door opens, and the people spill in. Everyone
knows exactly who arrived when, and just who they will
follow in line. One nurse, acting as a receptionist, immediately starts taking names, in order, and sending the first
few to the back. I'm seventh in line today.

The other six are out in a jiffy, talking a blue streak to
anyone within reach in the waiting room. This is one of
the most sadistic tricks imaginable. These saps are aching,
and they don't want to hear word one from somebody who
already got his. My name is called, just as I'm finishing
removing the third layer of skin from my index finger.

After my initial visit, I discovered soon enough that seeing the doctor himself was a rare occurrence, and that actually *getting hit up by him* was a privilege along the lines of a Papal benediction. The very day after that honor, the job of administering the "treatment" was assumed by a nurse. She was built like a porno star, and was operating on four-buttons undone down her crisp, white uniform. She proceeded with the injection with a professional yet loose-lipped touch. As she gently pressed a cotton swab to the point of entry and told me, in a fructose voice, to bend my elbow, I could have sworn she was going to lay a little peck on my cheek and hand me a lollipop. Instead she just wished me a fine day and gave her hair a toss which said, "Now piss off, honey. I don't bus no fucking dishes . . ." Yeah, and I'll bet she don't take no short orders either.

Since then, I've had my treatments handled by a rotation of three equally glib angels of mercy. All have the top four buttons undone, so I assume this is some edict from the man himself. All have the same gentle touch with a syringe. That seems reasonable, as far as mandatory occupational skills go. After all, it's the only thing they have to do.

After all the roof landings and burnt-out shells of tenements, it is an amazing feeling to be taken care of in this way. The sober footsteps, the sterile surroundings, the gleaming cabinets of glass and stainless steel, syringes used once then forever disposed of (I find *that* sad, sort of like seeing a pup doomed to be gassed . . . you just want to ask if you could possibly scoop it up and give it a good home), the Amazon nurses with stiff, starched whites head to toe, the degrees in prominent display next to lithos from the art pantheon (most probably clientele themselves), the waiting room filled with diamond-decked necks and lapdogs— surely this place is a glimpse into the future. In that respect, I find myself fearing it a little more each day. And today, the fear runs even higher. Today, the great doctor himself approaches me and escorts me into his office. It seems he's going to take care of me himself.

In his office, there is a petite tray of cold cuts and tomato slices. I eye it, more for the novelty of seeing food again than from any desire for something as crass as eating. Noticing this, he booms in his thick Slavic accent, "Ah, yes . . . my breakfast, you see. Are you eating properly? One must eat well for the treatments to be effective." A stunning notion comes to me: I mean, just what the fuck are we being *treated* for? I do feel a bit tired, however . . . how about that old, uh, shot there, Doc? The fact is that what we here are being treated for is the treatment itself. We are being made well daily for the mistake of coming here in the first place. All the rest is sanitary conditions, nurses revealing half a tit, and a fresh set of works. I happen to know that if your work takes you on the road, the doctor will put together a traveling kit for you. All you need . . . *sans* the half-tit.

The doctor asks me what I'm up to, sitting me down and adjusting the rubber tie above my vein. I tell him that I am on my way to New Haven, that I am giving a poetry reading at Yale tonight. "By the way, doctor," I add, seizing the opening I've just created, "do you think you could put a little extra *boost* in today's, uh, treatment . . . seeing about the reading tonight and all . . . I was, naturally, up to quite the late hour last night in preparation for this event which I look on as, well, something of an honor. Yale, being what it is and all that?" The doctor turns to me, a tomato wedge and salami slice pinched in an elegant manner between thumb and forefinger. He hesitates a moment, deciding if he should raise up the chow for consumption or give me a reply. "Yes, that can be done," he answers with his mouth full, having settled on doing both at the same time. "That will be no problem." I figure he's laying a placebo rap on me, but I'm made to believe when I notice him pull out of his stash cabinet a different-shaped bottle. It is also a different color, more orange than red. "The color of your hair, yes?" he remarks as he draws it up the tool of his trade. He seems to enjoy playing up the mad-doctor effect

produced by his Euro-East accent and these sudden bursts
of up-from-the-cauldron laughter. He reaches down and
injects, then tosses me a swab with the air of some field
marshal who actually had to *fire* a weapon himself. No
doubt about it, today's shot certainly came from a more
powerful batch, maybe from the old croaker's personal
stash. I tip off with a whole new attitude about the treatment and its validity as a vital, and all too essential force
for society in general and, specifically, this individual. I
swing out into the waiting room for some ebullient, sadistic
chatter with those lying in wait. "Doesn't this brisk air just
make you want to shout, 'It's good to be alive!'" I scream
into the throbbing skull of some poor woman with a hearing aid. "I just can't wait to get back out there and really
breathe, you know?"

So I open the expensive doors and am instantly greeted
by a tubular blast of wind which rams against my chest like
a telephone pole . . . as if it were literally tossed at me by
one of those Scottish guys that do that sort of thing. Worse
yet, it's beginning to snow and I catch myself speaking to
the flakes falling before me: "Ah, yes, we are all truly in-
dividuals." I reach down deep into some bare recess of
logic within a brain that feels like it's gyrating on an axis
like a classroom globe. Down there I grope around among
the topographical layers and, at the bottom of a small, gray
lake, I pull up the realization that I am, as of this moment,
a man not responsible for his actions. I notice a small scroll
unrolled on my thumb, covered with flotsam and gray
seaweed. It reads, "Take a cab . . . do not go anywhere but
home. Now."

I opted for this advice, wherever it came from. I signaled
a cab through the rapidly increasing swirls of snow. One
turned right up to the spot where my hand was waiting to
open the door. I thought that an amazing feat. I hopped
in and gave him the destination. He threw the flag and
took off, not knowing, not suspecting in the least, what he
had picked up and what he was in for.

CHRISTMAS WITH D.M.Z.

Christmas dawn. I am with my famed painter friend, and sometime employer, D.M.Z. It is 6:20 A.M. We're driving up the East River Drive, and the reading on the speed-ometer, 68 M.P.H., has nothing on either of us. Our brains and our tongues are moving faster than epileptic hum-mingbirds.

It began about two hours earlier. I had crashed at D.M.Z.'s loft the night before, prepared to assist him from the mo-ment of waking for what was certain to be a busy day, filled basically with the Christmas morn chores of any father of two girls, aged three and five, and the preparations for a party for the high-toned uptown/downtown set come night. So what do you do when it's 4:30 in the morning and so much lays in wait to be done? You each jab a syringe filled with a take-out dosage of Dr. Feelgood's amphetamine so-lution into your ass. You pack the endless parts of the jungle gym, which is another main gift for the kids, onto the freight elevator, plus sundry dolls, high-tech gadgetry and other stocking stuffers, all still unwrapped in the shop-ping bags from F.A.O. Schwarz, and lower yourself in the big, open platform down to street level. You squeeze it all into the artist's spitting-new El Dorado, and take them up-town to the apartment on the West Side where his wife and kids live, and assemble them into functional tools of child madness. A million daddies are doing the same this very moment all over this city (including the islands of Staten and Long). D.M.Z. and his wife, Samantha, have been sep-arated a year now. That's when she moved into the vast, old, high-ceilinged apartment of twelve rooms overlooking Central Park. I live there myself, since I work for D.M.Z. and his wife. I work in D.M.Z.'s studio some days, stretching canvas, taking works to framers and such. I also help Sa-mantha at the apartment, taking care of the domestic chores. (Okay, I *baby-sit!* Is there some problem you have with that?) It's a great gig for a young poet and I have the two small maid's rooms in the back, connected by my own private bathroom. I use one as a bedroom and the other as a studio to write.

I have plenty of time to write, and I enjoy walking the kids through the park, where I acknowledge the compliments toward my supposed progeny by old and young women alike with an aloof nod, gathering the two young beauties closer to my side with a protective pride. I walk them each day to the fountain at 72nd Street, where I feel like an American man, above suspicion and under the veil of innocence flanking me, right and left, three years and five, blonde and blonde.

Their mother Samantha is truly one of the most amazing people I know. We have a unique relationship. "Confederates" . . . that's the word for us. She is notoriously sexy, yet we have never made it together. I'm not sure where that would spring us. As the song says, "She's my best friend."

"So, do we have everything?" D.M.Z. speedily queries, the El Dorado buzzing beneath the off ramp of the Triboro Bridge.

"We got everything, as sure as I can tell," I answer with acceleration. All the parts to assemble the jungle gym . . . the envelope with the instructions. And all the other stuff we hid down there to prevent accidental discovery by the kids, thus seriously denting their belief in 'Father Christmas' (which, since their Mom is English, is their moniker for Santa Claus). The table Samantha needs for the party buffet is still at the studio, of course. "Is that a dead dog or cat ahead of us?"

"Dog," D.M.Z. replies with admirable monosyllabic restraint. "Why are we going this way, anyway?" I ask. "The apartment is on the West Side, and we got to get that fucking jungle gym up before the kids wake."

"Don't worry; it's covered," D.M.Z. shot back. "Samantha had the kids stay with their aunt last night . . . they won't be back until noon. By then Father Christmas and his helper will be done. Hand me the bag; I'm pulling over. Move quick . . . chop-chop."

We pulled over into an emergency parking spot, unzipped a shaving kit filled with syringes already loaded with the doctor's formula, crimson and measured, poked ourselves in the thigh, pressed the plunger and tossed the used works over the rail and into the Harlem River, where they joined a line of flotsam and condoms. We were back on the road within a minute, maybe less. It was like a pit stop in one of those auto races. It turned out the sole reason for this pre-dawn hop up the Drive was simply a matter of D.M.Z. joy-riding. He had just bought the El Dorado, a Christmas present for himself. When we hit the end of the Drive at Dyckman Street, my old neighborhood, we swung over to the West Side and got the other Drive down along the Hudson. It was strange, passing through those familiar streets just as the light was rising on Christmas Day. I wondered what my folks had planned for the holiday. I thought about it all the way down to Samantha's, then I folded it and dropped it beside the wheel of the El Dorado, double-parked in front of the building.

Armando, the doorman, helped us with the removal. We brought the stuff around the back of the lobby to the freight elevator, leaving the sizable parts of the jungle gym until last. Armando was, literally, puffed up with ecstasy. Christmas, after all, is the Feast of El Loaded Envelope for doormen, and he knew Mister Z. probably was good for the same C-note as last Christmas. Doormen have memories like gay elephants; he knew what sum lay behind every door in the building. If some family has a bad year, these guys are the first to know it and, come the holidays, the first to feel it. After we moved in the last section of the kids' main surprise, D.M.Z. laid Armando a straight-up $100 bill sans envelope, as we rose in the elevator. After everything was unloaded and the man went to ring the service bell, Armando whispered to me, "Shit man, that dude must paint some *big* motherfucking houses to make that kind of bread!" I agreed: "Him and Der Führer, no shit." Armando, a puzzled yet still joy-puffed face, shut the grate of the elevator and disappeared downward. Samantha came out and we moved all the things inside. She began wrapping the stuff that wasn't already gussied up while D.M.Z. and I began assembling the jungle gym. The pieces, laid out, made it look, to my eyes, a somewhat Herculean task.

"Donald Judd and Tony Smith couldn't put this mother together," I exclaimed.

It will be no sweat," D.M.Z. assured, "remember, I've done a bit of sculpting myself. But first let's hit the bathroom. Got the bag?"

I had it. We injected another "treatment," this time in the mainline. We went back into the dining room with a fresh, perspicacious take on the task at hand.

"First things first," D.M.Z. remarked, peering over the brain-drain, bring-down pile on the floor, "Let's check the instructions." I opened the envelope, loomed over them a moment, and looked again at the floor. There seemed to be more stuff than the time before. I was getting pissed off and paranoid, looking into the other room for a trickster.

"Now we're moving along," D.M.Z. stuck out his hand, "let me read those things. What's it say? You gotta know *how to read* these things. I have that kind of mind. You see, I work with *shape* . . . you're a writer, these things are difficult for . . ." "You read Japanese, then?" I handed him the paper. "Motherfuckers . . . and I got this thing at F.A.O. *Schwarz!*"

We went into the living room, sat down, took a Valium each and had a serious Marlboro. We needed a third person. We needed a listener. We called in Samantha. She consoled us awhile, then moved into the dining room. D.M.Z. and I didn't notice her leaving. We were both busy at the window with binoculars watching a teenage boy in his room in the high-rise across the street jerking off with a baseball mitt. "That's *wild*," D.M.Z. observed.

After we had finished watching the goings-on in every apartment across the street, mostly boring yule tide tableaus except for the two stewardess-types who were roller-skating in bra and panties around the living room table, snatching, as they passed, candy canes off the Christmas tree, we realized the time was approaching noon. Soon the kids would arrive . . . *and no jungle gym?* That's when we heard Samantha's soft British accent float in through the glass doors, "Yoo-hoo, could you give a hand, please?"

We entered the dining room. Shock. The entire gym was finished. Assembled. Right as any monkey bars in any playground.

"Now," she spoke, "All you need do is tighten the bolts, or whatever, on the things, then move it a bit over, so they don't burn themselves on the radiator as they climb. I'm going to get that layer of foam rubber to lay beneath it." And off she went. We were left to do what we were told.

The kids arrived just as the tree was lit and the gifts were laid out. They loved it all, especially the jungle gym. They were speeding in and out, up and down, making little chimp sounds. I wanted to join in, but didn't trust my weight. But this idyllic family scene couldn't last. D.M.Z. and I had to get down to the studio and pick up the sculpture, which functioned as a table, which was his own gift to Samantha. It was essential to get it up here ASAP so it could serve up the buffet for tonight's party. We grabbed the kit and went in the back to my room. We took care of business, *Hasta-luegoed* out the door, talking our way to the car.

On the way downtown, D.M.Z. began to suffer at the thought of transporting the sculpture/table. He had let all his assistants off for the day (except me, of course . . . but then again, I never could be called an actual "assistant." I was more like, well, a baby-sitter, okay?), and he had no access to the van which one of them owned. The only solution was tying it onto the roof of the El Dorado, and that didn't sit well with the man at all: his spanking new Caddy with six hundred coats of maroon paint being subjected to the humiliation (and possible dents and scratches) of performing the menial task of a "goddamn pick-up truck."

"The El D. ain't no beast of burden," he muttered repeatedly.

And the "table" was no ordinary breakfast-nook surface, either. It was, after all, *art*. It was huge. It was canary yellow, and worst of all, the shape made it outrageously cumbersome. If my geometric memory serves me well, I'd guess you'd call it a trapezoid. But these are the details you should not trust me on. I don't do no windows or research. I do load cumbersome, 200-pound canary-yellow trapezoids onto the roofs of Cadillacs, however . . . after the man has laid down about a dozen layers of padding beneath, that is. There was enough foam rubber there to provide luxurious bedding for six firehouses. D.M.Z. fastened it with rope himself. It was obvious he was placing the humiliation of the jungle gym fiasco right on me, and that my duties henceforth consisted of thoughtless manual labor. That was fine with me. I had plenty of nothing to think about with the buzz I was carrying. I walked a few doors down for smokes. From there the clashing of the maroon and yellow colors was just dreadful. D.M.Z. signaled me that all was secure. I hopped in and we headed uptown. At a red light I could see our reflection in an office building. It looked like there was a giant cockroach, dusted thick with some bright yellow insecticide, fastened on top of the car, feet-up dead position. As if we should have a sign on the door: "D.M.Z. Exterminators."

We double-parked, *déjà vu*, in front of Samantha's building. Armando the doorman had lost that puffed-up ebullience. Obviously, all the envelopes were in. Needless to say, he wasn't quite as helpful. D.M.Z. and I had to unload and carry the thing into the lobby by ourselves while Armando went off, muttering something about "fetching the freight elevator." (How does one "fetch" an elevator?) We laid the piece down in the lobby. It was there I really checked it out for the first time, set in its natural position. It *was* a terrific work, and I could finally trust my judgment on this because it had been awhile since my last shot of Feelgood's elixir.

Armando came back, obviously having fetched the elevator. D.M.Z. told us to wait there in the lobby, while he went and parked the car . . . not to move the work without him. I realized he himself thought of the thing as sculpture first, table last, and it was to be handled with the same care as the El Dorado. That meant under *his* supervision. I could dig that: even though the back elevator was enormous, this object was going to provide a challenge. It didn't have as many coats of paint as the car, after all.

"I saw we passed a spot right up on 74th Street," I offered.

"Yeah, I saw it. Sit tight. I'll be back in a minute."

"Wait," I yelled as he turned, "Take your coat. It's fucking freezing out, and you're all sweaty with just that pullover job."

"Umm, forget it . . . I'll be right back anyway." D.M.Z. turned again. I could see he was ripped. He must have snuck a solo shot at the studio. That was okay by me. I was feeling better without the shit at this point. But I suddenly recalled Samantha's exigent plea to retrieve her younger daughter's doll from the back seat of the Caddy. It was a ratty ragdoll she had had since the cradle; it served as a security object, and she was having a tiny, three-year-old breakdown without it. I ran out to the street, turned around the corner and up 74th, where I saw him a block away, shivering back toward me. The car was already parked.

"Get Ola's nanny!" I yelled. (Nanny was what she called the doll.) I was cold myself, and I was wearing a coat. I had his on my arm.

He signaled okay and turned back to the car. It looked

like he might be having trouble finding it and, besides, he needed his coat. So realizing what a jerk I was just standing there, I ran up to meet him. Meanwhile, he was coming back, waving the doll.

There was still half a block between us when an amazing scene took place. Two hefty cops sprang out from between parked VW buses and slammed D.M.Z. against the wall of the building. Though they were in uniform and their car was parked next to Mr. Z.'s, I had not noticed any of it until they sprang. It might as well have been out of thin (cold) air. One of them was cuffing D.M.Z., after a quick frisk, when I saw the other one charging at me. The perspective was strange. He was heading in such a straight line that, mixed with my cop-fear adrenaline, it appeared he was moving *backwards*. I just stood there, wondering why, not to mention how, he was doing this. Then the illusion broke. It broke at just about the same moment he grabbed me by my collar and upended me off my feet, assisting gravity with his arm's force, so that when I landed on the pavement, with the back of my head absorbing said force, *it really did hurt* . . . I'd say about twice as much as it would have had it not been for his assistance. Before my head cleared, I was cuffed. He was over me like a cheap hump, looking down, examining the bottle of Valium he had removed from my pocket. I must have been out for a bit. The other cop had D.M.Z. and was alongside us. The two bags of blue shit yanked me up off the pavement like some perishable litter. The cop saw that the Valium were legit, that the Rx matched the ID in my wallet, which he had apparently seized as well. What I was becoming quite concerned with, as the mist in my brain began to empty out my ear and the throb of the whack subsided, was the whereabouts of the kit filled with Dr. Feelgood's formula. I realized it was, in fact, a prescribed substance to D.M.Z., but I just could not accept this fact, out of habit or some covert moral whisperings. One thing was certain: legal or not, the cops were not going to fancy all those syringes

loaded with such an intriguingly red liquid. It would mean
a trip to the station for sure. I mean, things were not looking too well as it was; and I was just beginning to see the
whole scene from the cops' perspective. A middle-aged
man with longish, stringy hair winding down the back of
a thin shirt which, despite the fact that it is three degrees
out, has no coat over it. He is running from a brand new
Cadillac in boots which are spray-painted silver (Had I
mentioned that? Oh, yes, D.M.Z. had done it that very
morning after the first shot), and he is waving a rag doll
above his head in a gesture of apparent triumph. Waving
back to him is a twig-like humanoid with translucent skin
who has so much orange-colored hair hanging from his
head that if they stuck him in a garbage can and set this
mop on fire it would burn long enough to keep them warm
for approximately half of their eight-hour shift. Both of
these characters have pupils in their eyes that are big enough
to serve a litter of kittens milk on. On searching the sporty
sort with no coat, the cops find no identification, no wallet,
a ring of keys and $4,000 in cash. The other person (or
plant, or whatever) has a draft card in his wallet designating
him 4-F ("Shit, I wonder why?" cracks one cop) and a vial
of tranqs. The coatless guy keeps mumbling some shit about
Armando chipping the paint if he tries to move the table.

"You guys get in the squad car," one cop barks through
the wind. "We're going down to the precinct."

"What for?" asks D.M.Z., still holding the doll as he gestures wildly.

"Car theft, to begin with . . . then we'll talk about everything else," the cop replies, then turning toward me: "Is
that his coat? Give him his coat."

I give D.M.Z. his coat, still somewhat in a daze, but before
he can get it around his shoulders we are shoved into the
car. In the one short movement we are together in the back
seat alone. I ask about the Doctor's kit, but before he can
answer, the quiet cop is in the front seat behind the wheel.
The other one is quickly beside him, filling out some shit

in a thick pad as we drive off. My head is clear enough
now to realize we are arrested on Christmas Day.

"How's your head?" D.M.Z. asks. He is winking furiously,
looking like he's in a pre-seizure state. (I know about such
things: it has been my good fortune to know many epilep-
tics in my youth.)

"Not bad," I reply, "umm, are *you* okay?"

"Yeah . . . fine. Anyway, don't worry. You can always see
The Doctor. I left him at the studio." Wink. Wink.

Now I got it. How clever. He must have left the works
there when he took that last shot, the one he did alone.
Without telling me. I couldn't have been more upset. I
mean, where did he get off leaving the shit downtown and
out of reach like that? And after *he* had *his* shot and left
me hanging! I'll bet it was a big shot, too. In fact, he might
have even done up a double.

"You could have *consulted* with me!" I blurted out, not
realizing what I was doing. He looked at me with aston-
ishment. Both cops turned around. I thought quick. "About
my rights!" I yelled at the cops, indignation oozing onto
the seats, "I mean you guys did not consult me, nor, I
presume, my friend, on our rights. I demand you read us
that stuff you read . . ."

"Take it slow there, haircut." The driver cop spoke this
time, "You haven't been charged officially with nothing.
We just want some clearing up . . . some explanations."

"The whys and wherefores?" I added.

"Right. That's very good."

We pulled up to the station house. One cop led us in as
the other went to park. We were standing in front of the
incoming desk; the sergeant checking us out as the es-
corting cop handed him some papers. We were both still
cuffed, but now it was with our hands up front. D.M.Z.
was holding the doll. It seemed to offer him the same
security it did Ola. He had his long black leather coat draped
over his shoulders cape-like, giving him suddenly a sinister,
vampiric air. The desk sergeant clearly did not dig it. I

didn't think D.M.Z. realized exactly how menacing he looked in such a pose . . . as if he was about to fly up and fang the man any moment. So I eased over behind him and snatched the coat off. It slid down and over my cuffs, covering them as if I were a magician about to do an escape trick. D.M.Z. looked at me, thinking I was going off my skull again, like in the squad car. "You look like fucking Bela Lugosi," I whispered. "All the cops are looking at you like they're about to reload their pieces with silver bullets. The desk sergeant in particular is looking at you like you're responsible for the death of a close and beloved relative." D.M.Z. nodded. "This whole thing is bullshit. It's pissing me off," he said. He meant it.

It was right then D.M.Z. switched gears. Some veil of initial intimidation had lifted, and he took control with a vengeance. He walked up to the desk, asked what the purpose was behind us being dragged down here, and demanded access to a telephone. The old sarge looked somewhat taken back, as if he had not heard any words spoken from that spot without a Spanish accent for many, many years. He began to speak, but before he opened his mouth halfway, one of our two uniformed friends whisked the two of us off to a small, bare room on the second floor where two detectives were waiting. They took off the cuffs and had us sit. The uniform handed him more papers with the info he got from us at the scene and split.

The detectives were genial enough sorts, as far as plain-clothes cops go. They weren't, so it seemed, going to play that good guy/bad guy routine, or any other cop games. One guy's name was "Barney." I thought that was funny, but I was through laughing. D.M.Z. likewise, and more so. He had now totally recouped his wits. The whole scene, and the frozen air which he had suffered through it in, coatless, had evaporated the tender mercies and undue generosities of the drug. It was clear he had taken inventory of his own place in the scheme of things and the cops' relation to it. It wasn't some "famous artist" sense of vanity, or at least not totally. It was more a simple assessment of where he stood, and what his options were. *They*, after all, had dealt the cards.

That was what I saw in his eyes, so I was surprised at the polite manner with which he handled the cops' questions, which were pretty much all directed at him, which was fine by me. It was hot in the small room. I took off my coat. D.M.Z. still clutched the doll.

"What were you doing running from the car?" asked the detective. The other one had gone off, probably to run down our names.

"I was running because I had left my coat in the lobby of my building, which was just around the corner. Then I saw my friend had come out to bring it to me, and I wanted to get it. I wanted to put it on. It's cold out there, have you noticed? Your friends could have cleared all this up if they had just taken us to the lobby and asked the doorman . . ."

"What's with the doll? You like dolls, or is that your friend's thing?" The cop interrupted, clearly implying a homoerotic relationship was happening here somewhere.

"It's my daughter's doll," D.M.Z. answered, his voice was even and underlined with cool rage. There was no trace left of that amphetamine quiver. "I was bringing it to her. She had left it in the car, and my friend, *who works for me*, reminded me to get it. I went back for it. That's when your boys assaulted us."

"What do you mean he works for you?" The cop let D.M.Z.'s allegation of brutality slide, as if perhaps he'd heard it before. "What does this kid do for you? What's your line of work?"

"I'm an artist." D.M.Z. said upright. He didn't fold the way I do when I tell people that I'm a poet.

"An artist? Whatta you mean an artist?"

"I'm a painter."

"You make a *living* that way?" the cop asked, eyebrows

swiveling like his fat ass in his chair. The other cop came back in. He had a phone.

"I make a living that way, yes." D.M.Z. was curt. He eyed the phone.

"Uh, listen pal," the other cop spoke for the first time. His voice was high-pitched. It didn't fit his body. I didn't laugh.

"Umm . . . now, we got the line on '*artists*,' and they don't go around with $4,000 in cash, driving El Dorados, you know what I'm saying?"

"Some don't and some do," D.M.Z. answered. "I do."

"What about your wallet and ID? Where's the car's registration? I think your story is bullshit."

"Make a call, please?" D.M.Z. queried politely.

"Go ahead," the squeaky-voiced guy pushed over the phone, "You better have a lawyer on the other end."

I had no idea who D.M.Z. was about to call. I figured it would be Samantha. She could handle the details of lawyers and stuff. Then again, knowing him, he might be dialing the building's lobby to tell Armando not to scratch the table by moving it because it was really a work of art, not a table. He dialed. The cops were just outside, actually sharing the same smoke. I don't suppose you could ever accuse these two mopes of being on the take.

D.M.Z. reached the party he had dialed. He looked at me with a smile, but gave no indication of who it was he was calling. He simply identified himself to the person's wife, who had answered, and asked if he could talk with "him." The mysterious "him" arrived on the other end of the conversation, and D.M.Z. laid out a terse summary of events. It included my getting cracked on the head when tackled by the uniform, and the detective's smart-talk. D.M.Z. listened to the stranger's voice after completing his story, then calmly handed the detective the phone.

"He wants to speak to you," D.M.Z. cooed.

The dick put phone to ear, and within minutes was turn-

ing the slimy pink of a tropical fish. I could hear the voice
on the other end chewing out the receiver. The cop cupped
the speaking end and told his partner to go get the captain
immediately.

"What the hell is up?" the other guy asked, his voice was
rising to a straight falsetto. It built up on each word like
Lou Christie singing "Lightning Strikes."

"Just get the summa-bitch, haul ass," the taker of the call
replied in stage whisper. Every cop on the floor turned,
typewriters stopped. The dick hauled the phone back to
his ear. It was like he was pulling a corpse out of the river.
"Yes sir, the captain will be right here . . . no sir, they were
not, as far as I know . . . yes sir . . . yes, I do have the names
of the arresting officers, sir, though you do understand
that no actual arrest was made . . . the phone call was allowed as a courtesy . . ."

With the last remark a stream of heavy reaming came
out of the receiver at such volume the cop had to pull the
phone from his ear. It hung limp there until a feisty little
dude arrived, puzzled and outraged. I assumed from his
manner, and the supplications tossed his way by the menial
brothers, that this was the captain. He had a belly that made
it look like he was wearing a belt of veal sausages strung
together beneath his shirt. He gave D.M.Z. and me a short,
ferocious gander, then took up the phone dangling from
the flunky's hand.

"Yes, sir . . . Captain O'Bannon here," he spoke, sounding a bit tentative.

I could hear the same barrage of shit shooting out the
phone. I was just leaning over to D.M.Z. to ask who this
potentate on the line was when I heard the captain's final
address: "Yes . . . fine, *Senator*, I'll do that. Yes, Senator,
Merry . . . uh, rather, happy holiday to you too."

Oh, that's a gem, I thought. If I hadn't already begun
a new book of diaries, this would have made it essential.
It was obviously Senator Jacob Javits, a veteran politician
and big-time art collector. He collected D.M.Z., and they

were big pals. He was coming to the party tonight, in fact. I looked at D.M.Z. with admiration. It's nice to be friends with the puppet masters, calling them up and having them yank those strings on the loathsome and unreasonable.

Things broke fast and loose then. The captain had assembled a tiny line of the main characters which we swaggered down, receiving apologies coated in deep layers of shit. The captain asked about my head. He wanted to know if I wanted to be run over to the hospital. I declined. I just wanted some rest. They took us in an unmarked car to Samantha's building. D.M.Z. thanked the cop, who was telling him all the way over about how good the crayon drawings his kid brought home from second-grade art class were, and asking what kind of guy "the Senator" was. "He's a good guy to call when you're busted," D.M.Z. said.

In the lobby Armando was standing there alone, shuffling his envelopes and counting their insides for the eighty-fifth time. D.M.Z. grabbed him by the shoulders like a naughty child and begged him to tell him where the table/sculpture was.

"*No problema,*" issued Armando, "I move it with my cousin Ralph."

"Ralph?" I interjected for some reason. D.M.Z. gave me an angry stare. I grabbed the back of my head pitifully and rubbed the sizable lump, feigning disorientation.

"It is fine, really." Armando continued, "Your wife came down and asked about you. I told her you go out to park car and don't come back. I figured you drive off somewhere. She told us to bring it up . . . Ralph and I. We put padding around it and brought it up the back elevator. It would not fit through the doorway, but your wife said she needs it now to put on food, so we take door off hinges and so were able to fit in. By the way, Mr. D.M.Z., I left my tools up in the apartment. I will put door back on in the morning."

"You left the door off?" D.M.Z. asked, his voice strained and plain tired.

"I put it on first thing in morning," Armando's voice was ushering us to the elevator, "Your wife says it is okay, okay?"

We went up in the elevator. It occurred to me that this was the first time we had taken the front elevator over the course of this long day.

"I got four syringes I saved for tonight," D.M.Z. spoke. "I stuck them in a dresser. You want one?"

"Sure," I answered, my voice not as enthused as it should have been, "But I'm going to take a nap first."

We got inside the apartment. Samantha wanted to know where the hell we were. She was pissed. D.M.Z. gestured her to hold off for a minute and went over to check the table. He was all over it like white on rice, under, above, around and through. The paint was unscathed, and he seemed satisfied. I told them I was going in the back to my room to have a nap. Deborah Duckster, the debutante, my girlfriend, was arriving early for the party with our friend Sue. They were going to help Samantha with the food and stuff. I had to get some z's before they arrived. As I went into my bedroom in back, where at the end of the hallway the rear door that Armando had removed for the table/ sculpture's unscathed entrance was lying in a mess on the floor, I could hear D.M.Z.'s voice trailing off. It was sweet within pure cool. He sounded like a little kid: "Listen to this . . . wait until you hear what *happened to us* . . . wait until you hear what *I did* . . ."

The second my head made contact with pillow, I went into a leaden sleep. I had some dreams which I only remember now in tattered bits. They were, for the most part, strangely realigned playbacks of the day's stunning events. I remember most vividly the actual bust made by the cops. When the real thing went down, it all happened so fast and chaotically that I lost track of most of my feelings in the process. Now, in the dream, everything came back in slow motion. It was ten times as terrifying, and the cops were twice as big and three times as ugly. Worst of all, it didn't

have the same extraordinary ace-up-D.M.Z.'s-sleeve ending. In the dream, the last thing I recall was the two of us
on a train, our hands and feet fastened together with thick
chains. We were traveling upstate along the Hudson, and
throughout the entire journey we could see in the distance
our destination: a castle-like prison, as large as only dreams
can provide, with gun towers reaching into low clouds on
four sides, and we could hear the constant buzzing of black
helicopters which hovered over the various yards. Given
the exaggerated proportions of the buildings below, they
seemed like wasps at the entrance to their hive. God, were
those machines ever loud!

Across the aisle from us were two guys, also linked by
the shackles, heading toward the prison which seemed, by
their gleaming expressions, to be home. One looked like
George Raft; the other was staring at me, his face vacillating
between menace and lust.

I only remember the most fleeting snatches of the scenes
in the prison itself. It seems the population there referred
to me as "Lollipop." Thank God for the Senator. He's got
my vote from this day on.

When I woke, Deborah Duckster, the debutante, much
to my amazement, was lying beside me reading a book. She
asked me how I felt. I told her "fine." She brought me
some coffee.

"You know," I spoke in a somewhat aggressive tone, "you
really should be helping Samantha out for the party, and
not be ever-so-cavalierly reading a fucking book!"

"Is that so?" she replied, her mouth half sneer, half smile,
"and what party is that?"

"What are you, high or some shit?" I sprang up, "The
Christmas party of course . . . the big one. By the way, how
long before people arrive? What's the time?"

"It's ten o'clock," she said flatly.

"Well, shit . . . there should be people *here* by now. I got
to get dressed. You should have woke me."

"I did wake you . . ." Deborah returned, the anger

switching to her side of the conversation. "I woke you three
or four times. You were wasted. You just fell back out. It's
ten o'clock *in the fucking morning*, for God's sake. You slept
through the entire party. The kids were in here playing
with their deafening toy helicopters, and their dolls and
shit, and you didn't even stir.

"What kind of dolls?" I asked humbly.

"Who cares? What kind of question is that? If you must
know, they were those new dolls you see in TV ads . . . the
ones with tongues that actually *lick*. They talk too. You pull
a string on their back and they say, 'I want lollipop.' They're
cute. Why?"

"No reason," I answered. "You mean I missed everything?"

"Yeah," Deborah said in a forgiving tone, falling next to
me on the bed, "What a drag you are . . . you miss all the
excitement. Oh! Listen to this . . . I met Senator Jacob Javits last night! He was here at the party with his pretty wife.
He's quite a nice person."

"You can say that shit again," I spoke, pulling her giggling body in to me, "He's jake with me. Heh! Get it? *Jake
with me*. That's a pretty good one!" And if it's not, I'm too
delirious to know.

DUMPED BY RADIANCE

Deborah Duckster, the debutante, is putting the dump on
this boy here, denuding me, leaving me with nothing but
the dubious distraction of forced alliteration. I've spent the
day in bed, humping the knots of hatred we wove into the
sheets. Some emissary of madness is shoving a letter in my
ear, and I hear something like a man whistling to his dog,
precise and unceasing. I hurt all over, but my stomach has
outwitted all other pain. It feels like a strip mine run by a
corporation with unlimited resources . . . their machine op-
erators happy in their work, indefatigable, hungry for
overtime . . . wonderful benefits and a fine pension plan.

They'll be tearing away for a long time, and the only thing they're looking for is bottom.

I'm not going to dignify any third parties with descriptions or rancor. I'll just say that the only thing she was modeling on her "working" trip to the Virgin Islands was a pearly camisole for some chump whose mind makes him eligible for handicapped parking. Besides, I've just been too stoned to notice; too stuck on freeze to care. I realize now the horror of such radiant features when their pretty facades are stripped away. They have the wrath of minor gods, vicious as rabid Dobermans.

I know I have only made reference to Deborah in the context of anecdotes . . . ("Context of anecdotes," hmmm . . . that sounds like something Alice would find written on a door in Wonderland) . . . but I've only avoided writing about her in depth because I was blinded to a point of incapacity by that radiance. I watched a lot of great women, whom I knew even then had more to give me, coming and going, walk out of my reach as I was pinned down, arms, eyes, and groin, by the pressure of Deborah's light, her perverse, orphaned light.

This is one of those times when being addicted to a drug seems a blessing. I don't have to go through the inane posturings of some dilettante afraid to insert an equalizer for fear he is doing it only to "escape." Fuck, I'd be getting off now out of pure physical necessity, even if this jilting bag and I were cruising the Aegean on our honeymoon. I suppose all there is left to do is get on with the job. You draw up your ego not from stains on a black satin sheet, but from the precision of the poem within . . . the torturous, elegant process of each clean, white page fulfilled.

A BAG OF FRUIT

I returned to the church I discovered last month. Its shape is somehow as soothing as its brilliant silence; long and narrow. The sides are lined with small grottos where crescent rows of candles burn before the statues of various saints, many of them rather obscure. Today I deposit a pair of quarters in a small brass box, light a candle before the life-sized image of St. Jude, the patron saint of hopeless causes, and sit in the pew beside it. I play with the idea of prayer, but quickly lay the notion aside . . . like a package I have set on my lap as I sit, then place beside me. It's not because of its weight; the package is quite light, actually. It's more its shape . . . there are so many angles, so many edges beneath the thin wrapping paper. I don't know how to hold the thing. I don't know the bottom from the top. So I lay it beside me on the tan wooden surface, and let it settle as it will. By itself.

I am being overtaken by that strange sensation again: when my ears ring mildly with the sounds of the traffic passing, and there is a vaporous light outlining the bodies of strangers passing in daylight. Park Avenue South seems like a tunnel as I walk in the twilight to Max's, and I develop a passion for inhaling the fumes of buses when they halt to pick up passengers, the driver gunning the engine as he waits in neutral. I've gone through these periods before. The symptoms, allowing for minor variations, are the same. They seem to come more often lately. There is no warning. The sensation sneaks up, nervous and quick as an inexperienced purse-snatcher. The worst thing is it seems to come from someplace *outside* of myself, as if through a window which I thought I had secured long ago. I have searched myself throughout, shining as much light as I could manage within each shadowy recess. It's turned up empty. Maybe I should begin seeing my former shrink Dr. Menza again, but I suppose I burnt that bridge when I flipped him off after he wrote me out of the draft.

When I left the church after a couple of hours, I saw a horrible car accident at an East Side intersection. Some Buick ran a red light and a cab doing close to fifty swerved and lost it and went right through the window of a dress shop. The driver was dead on impact; his fare was taken off in an ambulance.

Violence is so terribly fast . . . the most perverse thing about the movies is the way they portray it in slow motion, allowing it to be something sensuous . . . the viewer's lips slightly wet as the scene plays out. Violence is nothing like that. It is lightning fast, chaotic and totally intangible.

I noticed the intense light surrounding the ghoulish on-lookers grow blinding. I noticed the fruit dealer directly across the intersection. I was watching him before the accident went down, weighing a bag of some fruit, in the shadow of his veranda, on an old-fashioned hanging scale. I continued to watch him throughout, by means of the peripheral vision I had perfected during my basketball years. He never looked up, not even with the hideous, metallic sound of impact, nor during the literal rain of glass shards landing within ten feet of where he stood. He simply watched the bag of fruit jolt the scale's needle to and fro until it finally settled, then proceeded to figure out the price with a thick black pen on the back of the paper bag itself. That's how long the whole accident took . . . the time it takes to weigh a bag of fruit. And he never even looked up, not even to see that the woman who had been buying that fruit had already walked away, moving in quick short steps, her hands pressed up to her eyes.

THE LOFT PARTY

Went tonight to an open bash for the denizens of the poetry and painting scene at the loft of Mike Goldberg. Mike is a generous dude, somewhat smooth around the edges. I don't mind the rumors; anyone who had his birthday celebrated in a long poem by Frank O'Hara is jake by me.

His loft is actually the gymnasium of an old YMCA building on the Bowery. The hoopless basketball backboards hang bright white, like minimalist sculpture, from an ap-

paratus connected to a slanted running track surrounding
the giant space. He's made a small equipment room on the
side into a posh bedroom. It's nice. Tonight it will be filled
with coats.

I meet up with Ted at Anne's. We smoke endless joints
of powerful dope and check out the new Van Morrison
album. That dude is hard to figure, for me at least. Everyone else swears by him. When I'm straight, eighty percent
of what he does is narcoleptic finger-popping time, but I
smoke a little grass and he's a genius, cut after cut.

When we finally arrive the place is literally quivering
from bodies dancing. The bass on the stereo system, which
Mike had borrowed from some musician friend, is throbbing so deep it has the effect of an acute packing of the
old fudge. We may have been rolling up close to three
years into a new decade, but in this cavernous place, the
sixties have not been cut loose . . . the music . . . the Looks.
It even smells sixties, what with the horrible, sweet berry-
like incense wafting about.

There was even rumor of some acid punch, but having
finally located it, the fake Steuben bowl was quite bare,
much to Ted's disappointment. I would have passed anyway. I've settled on the fact: acid is a marked deck and
each card's dealt right off the bottom. And the bottom was
too often where I went. I've assembled a nice head tonight,
without any preconceived formulations. Best not to exceed
chance perfection through greed.

I do, however, step over and help myself to some of that
fancy soft cheese with half a dozen layers of plastic you
have to peel off the top. As far as dispensing goes, you
can't beat Cheez-Whiz, and I say as much to our host. He
gives me a man's man chortle. I don't know . . . I like the
man, despite the rumors.

Everybody's here, and it's funny seeing all the uptown
swells and the downtown hotshots mixing it on the dance
floor of what is, in fact, a gymnasium.

"It's like the prom I never went to," I say to Ted, shouting over the butt-fuck bass.

"Ha, I never went to mine either," Ted replies, "Just one more addition to things we have in common, you and I . . ."

"We're Catholic," I throw in.

"We're guys," Ted adds.

"We're great," I state off-handedly.

"That's right," Ted agrees, "Heh, did you vote for *Eisenhower*?"

"I was about two years old, for Christ's sake."

"Oh, yeah . . . well, we fucked up there."

"Wait a minute," I jump. "Are you talking about his first or second term?"

"Second term," Ted issues hopefully.

"Oh, yeah . . . in that case," I answer, "definitely . . . I mean he won us the fucking war, no shit!"

"Fucking A."

There are some great-looking women shaking on the dance floor. I actually feel loose enough to frug it up a bit with Iris. Her pretty violet eyes. She's a ballet dancer, and they usually look horrid when they dance to rock-and-roll. But Iris is a torrid exception: she breaks point and shakes her ass. The only thing is, she's also one of those women who break into hippie-type Sufi dance bullshit and wind up free-flowing to the other end of the floor while you're still where you started, holding your dick while you do some idiot diddy-bop routine and looking like a fucking jackoff, hyper and partnerless. People start to point. You pretend you dropped something . . . bend down and make it to the bar.

Which is where I meet, naturally, Terry Southern. He's a funny guy. I like him, in spite of the fact that after working two full years of high school at getting my dick inside the family crest of this lovely, wonderfully precocious teenage actress I was going with . . . after spending inordinate (and I would not make money an issue if it were not in-

ordinate) sums of money on her . . . money which had been
previously allocated for mind alteration. . . . After all this,
who else but Terry Southern winds up performing the
hymen maneuver on her when she goes up for the lead in
the film version of his sicko-smut (I say this in a non-pe-
jorative sense) epic, *Candy*. You see, what you must realize
is that I had just about gotten there when said maneuver
took place. I was a weekend and one layer of vaseline away
from consummating what was, for me, a sweet, valid puppy
love. I had already had my dick in her mouth, in her hands
(both hands), her ears, her feet . . . those smoothly pedi-
cured and deep, red-painted toes . . . all these places and
more, and she, with that agile concentration peculiar to
New York girls, had had every extremity I had to offer
(except, alas, one) between her legs. This girl had a body
whose *blush* brought me to spasms. And *he*, this purveyor
of porn, gets her on a casting couch at first callback in an
office in Midtown, the oldest gambit in the business of
show. Beaten out by a *social satirist*, my Lord.

We laugh about it now. We laugh about it tonight, in
fact. He seems to laugh harder, however. And last.

But wait . . . who is this familiar-looking elderly man with
the three-piece suit approaching Terry with impeccable
dignity to offer greeting? Good Lord, it's Mr. William S.
Burroughs, and Terry is ushering him to my side of the
bar table for an introduction. Burroughs shakes my hand
and asks for some vodka-based cocktail. He actually uses
the word "cocktail." He thinks I'm the fucking *bartender*,
for God's sake. This immediately presses the wrong button
in me, since I come from three generations of mixologists,
and I like to think I have taken enough pains for it not to
show. Anyway, Terry deftly starts mixing the drink for Mr.
B., and I take the close-up opportunity to check him out.
Surprisingly, he offers me an apology for the mix-up.

"It's okay," I speak up, startling myself with my own
casual air. "Actually, my old man, and his old man, were

bartenders. My grandfather owned a speakeasy up in Harlem during Prohibition. My old man was bartender. They were doing so well, in fact, that they began running some beer on the side . . . to parties for the swells and all that . . . My old man drove the truck. One night he gets stopped by two dudes. He figures they're Feds, and makes the designated offering. But the one guy laughs and tells him to put his money away, then to get in their car. It turns out they're goons for Dutch Schultz, and that's where they take him, to meet *the man* himself." I pause to see if I'm going over at all. I know, of course, that Burroughs has a fascination with Dutch Schultz. I'd read about it in an interview. But the story is perfectly true.

I simply can't believe I'm standing here, brightly conversing with the one literary idol of mine whom I had yet to meet. It's as if at twelve years old I was shooting hoop by myself in the playground and Elgin Baylor sauntered over and asked me if I wanted to go one-on-one.

"What happened?" Burroughs asked. He actually *replied*.

"Well," I turn it on again, catching myself before I lay my hand on his shoulder and call him "Bill," "what happened is (I'm switching tenses as if I'm pacing between two rooms) they did, indeed, bring him to the Dutchman, who is sitting behind a teakwood desk in an office in back of some dive . . . my old man knows who it is, and is shitting in his . . ."

"Teakwood?" Burroughs interrupts cryptically.

"Say what?" I look up, disoriented. I realize I can't make eye contact and am telling the story to my drink.

"The desk was teakwood?" Burroughs clarifies himself.

"Yes, I believe that's what my old man told me," I nervously speak, thinking any second Mr. B is going to pull out some hideous weapon from the arsenal of his writings and exclaim, "Ha . . . you sniveling little shit liar . . . I happen to know, *a priori* as a fact, that Schultz's desk was *mahogany* . . . now extend your jugular, be hung by this strange device I have personally designed, and die, shitting and cumming in your pants, you purposeless slime of reptile egg!"

"Hmmm . . . that's interesting," Burroughs stated calmly. "Yep . . . that's just what I'd picture."

"Yeah, teakwood it was . . ." I quickly went on, sweating into the dip. "So Dutch Schultz says to my old man, 'Kid, we hear you've been running beer in my territory. Well, you're gonna keep running it, but from now on, you'll be running it for me, Dutch Schultz!' And so my father did, until after Prohibition. Then he got his own bar, legal."

"Schultz was mainly into *policy* anyway," Burroughs said, as if we were in fact talking *together*. "He didn't get stung as bad as some of the others after Repeal . . . just a matter of transition. And the Dutchman knew transition."

"Yep, never put all your eggs in one basket," I blurted out, realizing how utterly stupid it sounded the moment it dropped downward off my lips. I should have quit while I was ahead, I thought. By this time, Burroughs was swamped with hordes bearing greetings. I faded to a bench to sit. On the way, I passed Iris on the dance floor. It was funny. She leapt right in front of me, still moving furiously, as if we had never separated, as if we were dancing together all that time.

"I'm beat, Iris," I told her feigning breathlessness, "I gotta sit." I found a seat as she spun off, still into the Sufi-shuffle.

I check things out alone from higher up, having climbed the spiral steps to the running track. I'm sitting on the edge, feet dangling, my position so much like a standard camera-angle for scenes that everything below becomes stock footage.

Except Burroughs, who I key in on. Like some painting at the Frick, you need the right distance to take him all in . . . to appreciate his overall presence, his specific features. With those long, elegant fingers, the aristocratic nose (which appears never to have been broken, which for some reason surprises me), the head tilted upward, Lord, the man is the image of Sherlock Holmes. Even from up here I can hear that voice, like a low-key carnival barker. It's like freshly split wood, clear, clean, but loaded with splinters.

He's here from London, but I don't know what for. I hope he does some readings while he's here. I'd like to know what he's doing these days. To tell you the truth, I've never been able to get into all that cut-up technique stuff. It may be pure selfishness on my part, but I want the story straight, like *Junky* and *Naked Lunch*, with all that obliterating passion and spiteful truth. I don't want that wisdom, unobtainable elsewhere, cut up into pieces, so that Chance might bring some faint revelation. When you rely totally on chance, you wind up with too much control. It's a safe way to play it. But shit, we *all* do that, and without having been anywhere near the zones where Burroughs has been, body and mind and, well . . . soul. But I read this volume of interviews with the man, and I don't want all that intelligence *realigned*. Not from him. Look at him. He's got the only eyes I really wanted to look into. And when I had the chance, I couldn't do it.

Ted comes over and we smoke a joint. It's been a while since I've smoked grass, and it's been unexpectedly pleasant tonight. Somehow I've avoided the paranoid winds that have been blowing up my streets lately. Maybe it's this sixties atmosphere. There was more of a sense of unity then, and I can feel it now. There was a certain comfort in those days, with all the goings-on. You had to move closer to each other; you had to hold on tighter. Lately everything spins away. Day to day . . . shit, I don't know where I'm gonna wind up. My housing situation is ludicrous. I'm worse than that other infamous moocher of bed and board, Rainer Rilke, the way I move from one friend's apartment to the next. I should split, but this city is like a lodestone, and I'm a tin motherfucker.

"You okay?" Ted asks, noticing I'm spaced.

"Yeah, I'm fine," I assure him, "I'm just stoned is all. I haven't smoked dope in a while."

"Okay," he says, "You look like you had a bellyache or something there for a second. Heh, lookit there . . . It's Allen and Peter . . . and Peter's got his *utensils*."

Indeed, Allen Ginsberg is over near the door with his long-time cohort Peter Orlovsky. The circle back to the sixties is now complete. Seeing Allen and Peter together brings a wave of Buddhist calm to my Catholic edge. Ted goes off to check things out downstairs. I start my camera rolling again, and the movie begins.

Close-up on Peter who, as Ted mentioned, has his utensils around his waist. He's wearing one of those telephone repairman-type belts, the kind with compartments to hold everything. But all they hold is a bunch of rags, in every size and texture. And on his hips, like Colt 45's, hang two of those small net bags (the type that oranges are packaged in) each containing two bottles of Windex.

It's clear Peter's on one of his methedrine jags. Allen recently purchased a farm in upstate New York to keep him off the shit, and allow other poets and friends to clean out there as well, but it seems that Peter (on his return to the city) has fallen to the deep persuasion of his drug of choice. Like I said, this place is a lodestone, and its reach is as long as all our doomed desires.

When Peter's on speed, he has one very simple mission: to clean everything in the world. And that's exactly the task he's setting himself to right this moment. He's beginning with the small kitchen area our host had installed, furiously attacking the door of the refrigerator, then the cabinet-space beneath the sink, proceeding up to the sink itself. (I hadn't noticed it from my previous angle, but the large loop in the back of his belt contains an economy-size can of Ajax, "the foaming cleanser.") People are astonished, but it's obvious there is no stopping the man, and nobody's trying. Why should they? It's a noble undertaking.

I close my eyes and set the camera into fast motion. Peter

is moving through Times Square, leaving everything behind him so clean you can hear the bottoms of Converse and Adidas squeaking as the brothers walk. Some people have taken off their shoes altogether, so as not to leave a mark, as if they were entering a Japanese restaurant.

I see Peter finishing off Manhattan . . . King Kong's fifty-year-old blood cleansed from the Empire State Building . . . the torch of the Statue of Liberty brighter tonight from its buffing with Windex.

Then, outfitted in an aqualung holding vast mixtures of oxygen and gaseous methedrine, Peter dives to the floor of the Hudson, near-fatally polluted, and begins vacuuming. It's all sucked in through a giant nozzle: century-old condoms, toxic waste congealed into strange pinwheel-shaped organisms creeping crab-like across the bottom, cars and trucks (whole or in parts, abandoned off piers each year for their outmoded luxury), mob rats with their proverbial cement necklaces, their rotting flesh still giving up bits of information to the fish.

But I can't keep the camera in focus any longer, and when I open my eyes the loft is almost empty. Ted is signaling me to come down . . . come down indeed.

Anne is still here. She says everyone went up to Ratner's to eat, and suggests we join them. We decide to walk up the Bowery, always a mistake, but worse now that I'm grass-high. The bodies are either sprawled on the sidewalk, freezing with no way or intention of fighting the cold, or keeping warm by snatching at us either for spare change, or because we're sober enough to be abused. Ted and I flank Anne and swing out to keep the boys clear. Their faces are blotched, toothless and swollen. It's the Middle Ages. It's New York City. It's a truly fucked situation.

We cross the street but it's worse, so we wind up walking in the middle of the street, right along the double-yellow line, until we pass Houston.

Ratner's is packed. There're three long tables pushed together in the back to accommodate the crowd from the party. By good fortune, Ted and Anne and I are seated with Ginsberg and Peter (who seems content to let Ratner's remain grime-ridden, concentrating instead on his soup), and Mr. Burroughs. Since I've already unloaded my Dutch Schultz saga, there is nothing I got to say. So Allen and Bill and Ted and Anne talk, and I watch. And I listen. I listen and I watch. Even while I eat, I listen. Watch.

A SUSPECT SENSATION

I've cut down the bags of dope I'm shooting daily, draining off the excess, but keeping well. Warding off the sickness symptoms . . . the sneezing, the flashes of quick transfer between hot and cold . . . the dancing bowels . . . I hate the litany. The point is, I'm measuring proper amounts to avoid all *that*, yet avoiding, at the same time, tripping into that vanishing point ready on the horizon, the nod. My mind begs to reach it. For now I'm keeping control, a feat only made possible by a steady connection, a non-user bestowed with a *latino* pride which prevents him from varying the quality of his goods from load to load, week to week. I am thus able to decrease my portion, day to day, without the count being rigged by some whack-happy, fly-by-night street dealer who is generous to a fault because of his inept basic math.

But despite all this figuring to keep well, there is a strange sense of desperate longing which overcomes me almost daily, and always around evening. It is a sensation not just of the somewhat sobering mind I am operating from— its force is physical as well. It is as powerful as a grappling hook, yet somehow delicate . . . a mild, yet unyielding persuasion. I feel this deep yearning as something that comes slow and exquisite, yet surely sinister, like a day-old, menacing laugh that overcomes me, too often in the most inappropriate places—public places, like at the ballet with Edwin Denby, or the back room at Max's, where I was, in fact, tonight, hanging upright for a change with the amphetamine gangsters of slime. When it comes it brings an overload of short, smooth questions. I feel my mind, separated from my heart, collating each question. I physically feel my brain absorbing them, like thin shreds of yesterday's newspapers in an awkward kitten's box. Maybe the cause is simple . . . that I am just letting down the shields I have constructed with such precision and care within each level of emotion and desire. But I am haunted by a horrible notion: What if this sensation (which is a handy but inaccurate word for it) comes from *outside*? I am heading up to the long church to think that over. Right now.

SOMETHING OUTSIDE

I need to confront last night's nagging notion that this sensation of unfulfilled yearning which I have experienced during my latest jag to cut down on dope comes from something (or someone?) somewhere *outside* my body, rather than from within. I can always somehow manage the latter, or bullshit myself into believing I can. This elusive force is something else. If I don't know where it's coming from, then I don't understand its source. If I don't understand its source, then I can't, and surely don't care to make any deals. It's frightening proposition time. I have a feeling like I'm drawing back a thick bow in my lungs, yet there are no arrows to shoot and I have no target anyway. I begin to realize the direction where my thoughts are heading, and I don't like the drift.

Though it's far, I walk to the long church, arriving just as a hearse is pulling away from the sidewalk out front. I'm glad for my timing, for once. I've sat through four funerals of total strangers while I waited, as if on line for a movie, for the place to empty and the silence to return. I enter and genuflect in a "When in Rome, do as . . ." manner. This place has some neat architectural tricks happening inside. It truly seems longer every time, as if some overzealous workmen were adding yards on at night in the small hours. New yards filled with new grottos filled with more and more saints, framed by racks of red candles. It's like a labyrinth in a single, straight line . . . as if old Zeno himself had drawn up the blueprints.

I notice a young priest step out of the side door. I realize that he is the first off-duty priest I have seen in this place. I want to talk with him, discuss the history and seeming mysteries of this place. I try to get his attention by waving my hand, not wanting to yell out crassly. He is moving too fast to notice, and disappears out the front door with a surplice slung over his shoulder like a dinner jacket and the swagger of a man stepping out on the town. I step outside to find him, but he's gone.

I light a candle midway down the right aisle, in front of the statue of an obscure saint named Dustan, who I find out later is the patron saint of lighthouse keepers. I step up to the row of candles to make my offering. I don't know if I should take it as an omen, but the fresh wooden taper will not catch on the flame I am using to get a light. It falters through many attempts, until it finally ignites and I pass it on to the virgin wick of my votive. I take my seat under the plaster blue eyes of St. Dustan, who it turns out was also heavy into politics and writing hymns, one of which was quite a hit on the Gregorian charts. His thin lips have an annoying hard-red tint to them, causing me to turn away, put total focus on the tabernacle.

Is it only the silence that makes me feel more lucid here? I don't know, and I don't want to get into that again. I'll take any shred of clarity where I can get it for now, figure out what happened later. I've decided this longing which I have been experiencing is of some outside origin. The shrinks can cringe all they want at that notion, but I'm feeling it and I know by now the limits of my traumas. This thing comes on like a voice, and it is surely not any muse. So am I talking demons? Possessors? I don't know. For now I am marking it down under the generic tab of evil, and the fact is I've never really had a problem with the idea that evil exists all by its lonesome: a self-contained force. Is that so hard to accept? Take a calm look in any direction. Now. The recent past. It's obscene to think the lames of this century were capable of inflicting such malice and suffering by their own devices. It's the biggest boast we can make, not admitting there's some other hand in the game, dealing off the bottom, middle and top. We haven't evolved nearly enough to lay down such overwhelming chaos.

THE NEW ORDEAL

I've tried in these writings to put a lid on the seamier side of the double life I've continued to lead—I am speaking, of course, of the street life as opposed to the art scene. The need for heroin has never allowed me to sever these ties. Besides, after all these years, there is a certain comfort in the familiarity of the streets . . . a fascination, even some perverse safety in its danger and lies.

Since Miguel got his head bashed in by the dealer we tried to rip off last night, I've tried to reconsider my immediate plans for the future . . . or non-future. I can't shake the cringing notion that it could have been me, not Miguel, who walked into that hallway first. So this morning, I popped over to the drug emporium of Avenue C., scored six bags, enough to last until tomorrow, and made a few phone calls. I called Stanley K., my old high-school pal, and took him up on his offer to ask his doctor papa to put the word in for me at his resident hospital and vouchsafe me immediate passage onto the methadone program there. Stanley turned out with his usual efficiency, calling me back within the hour and telling me to get my ass right up there—a certain Mrs. Toto would be waiting to enroll me in, as Stanley calls it, The Academy of the Future.

The hospital is on the fringe of Spanish Harlem. I'm not giving out the name, but Moses saw a burning bush there once . . . I think it was in the emergency clinic while he was

waiting for attention. I shouldn't joke—this is a break. I
can't hack the bullshit in the streets anymore. The dope
sucks lately and the dealers are worse. I can't live my life
any longer on the dealer's time, waiting on cracked stoops,
passing through the streetlights of SoHo, or swinging on
the monkey bars in the Pitt Street Park, frozen in winter,
my tongue stuck to the metal in anticipation. Waiting, always waiting, for the man to arrive. He knows you'll wait—
there is no alternative. So that's what I need, and that's all
this will be—an alternative, something along the lines of
stability and regularity. It's my only choice for my work. I
need a consistency in my moods if there is to be any consistency in my style. I can't attempt to write always in the
hollow flux of desperation and incipient terror. I try to
cover this up, cower behind some facade of humor, hoping
that old Aristotle was right—that humor will act as a catalyst
to purify the tragic. But it can't go on. My body is broke.
I'm shitting where I eat.

So I arrive in this cavernous building and wander through
the maze of corridors in search of the methadone clinic
and the awaiting Mrs. Toto, whom I picture as being either
from the Orient or Oz. I finally find the place, as I imagined, in some basement far from the adjacent big-money,
Fifth Avenue-endowed pavilions. It's right around the bend
from the two swinging doors of the morgue.

I enter the clinic through an imposing-looking door. The
hours during which the medication is dispensed are marked
on a sign which is painted a sickly yellow, not unlike the
jaundiced color of hepatitis, and a woman, quite attractive
and not Oriental, greets me. She leads me into a small
cubicle of an office, where I sit down to answer questions
for the seemingly endless pile of forms and releases.

There is a glass door, so I can see out into the clinic
itself. A Puerto Rican guy and his old lady are having a
mild disagreement in a corner next to a tank of tropical
fish. There is a nurse behind a bar, not unlike the small
partition of an Orange Julius stand, handing a cup full of

measured liquid to a black dude with a shaved head. Mrs. Toto finishes with the more formal data and moves on to some quasi-psychological tests—old standards like the ink-blot, etc. I keep getting distracted by the couple in the corner arguing. Their gauges are moving toward red. Now I have to draw a picture of a tree—God knows what it has to do with anything. All I want is some of that orange shit in the paper cup. I draw the tree and reveal more about my lack of draftsmanship than the condition of my mind. I draw it totally barren of leaves, with dead branches twisted and gnawed like the fingers of a cartoon witch. I imagine they'll conclude from this that I am a sick, empty spirit, but it's just that, from the first days of second-grade art class in the School of the Good Shepherd, I have never been able to draw a leafy tree. The barren trees of fall were always my specialty. The only thing the picture reveals is the condition of my education. But shrinks, prigs that they are, will not consider this point and will have a proper field day profiling me from a sketch of a fucking tree. Jung would be outraged. I hand the drawing and the box of crayons back to Mrs. Toto, who is half-standing and craning her neck to see out the window into the clinic.

I can hear, as I turn, muffled screams. My God—it's the Puerto Rican couple. The guy is holding the girl by the nape of her thin, brown neck and pushing her head down into the water of the fish tank. I see her face through the glass, her eyes like they are about to explode in the water and he is not yielding a bit. A security guard rushes in and pins the guy. She doesn't realize, for a moment, that he has let her go and just stays underwater in frozen terror. Her chin is pressed into the colored shards of gravel on the bottom. Guppies and black mollies are in panic and grouped in the corner, gyrating in what resembles some sort of mating ritual. There is a green fern sticking in the poor girl's ear like a rancid Q-tip. The nurse pulls her head out and a barbed swordtail slides from her hair onto the floor. I scoop it up and flip it back into the tank. The senorita is gasping for air and, at the same time, going for her boyfriend's privates with the tip of her boot. The guy, being held by the guard, catches one in the left testicle. It's mayhem all over, nurses diving to contain this half-drowned ball of fire. I get escorted to the door, pulled away from the fish tank where I'm trying to ascertain the damage to a Siamese Fighting Fish which seems severely disoriented. Maybe they should have it draw a tree.

Mrs. Toto, at the door, gives me a polite shove and tells me I can start tomorrow morning on the mojo juice. I can't believe my good fortune . . . this place is a veritable bedrock of rehabilitation.

SOMETHING WORTH THE WATCH

New York has become like a used car held together by K-Y and coat hangers; I've been thinking about unloading it and trading it in for something with cleaner angles . . . maybe California deserves a chance. A lot of poet friends have abandoned the squalor of Alphabet City and the Lower East Side for the bovine whines of this little coastal town outside San Francisco. I need a more controlled environment; I need to put the brakes on all this excess and all these variables. The only certainty in my life these days . . . these years, more accurately, is uncertainty: the uncertainty of rising with the late sun twisting through broken blinds and the echo of sirens. I can differentiate the wail of ambulance from police car from fire engine from the final scream marked "Civil Defense."

It's a dream, a nightmare since birth . . . Berlin, and the missiles in Cuba that foggy October. They were never dismantled in my gray subconscious.

I walk the streets aimlessly, mugging my own depression with the quick and ephemeral. Only the lines of architecture against the shadowed sky in midtown calm me down, so I search like a thief for the edges of buildings, sharpening themselves on sunlight.

I can't throw up that hackneyed shit about "getting back to the land," because I've never been there in the first place. But I am beginning to long for the cave in the back of my memory . . . with a desk, a dog and a fire. Summer or winter or both, it doesn't matter. I just need something there, worth the watch, from one day to the next.

TERROR IN THE LOBBY

I have this abscess in the pit of my right forearm. It's been there for about a month now. I've been on the methadone program much longer than that and, since I haven't used any needles since I got on, it didn't come from a missed shot, or bad dope. The doctor at the program said it's just a delayed manifestation of continuous wear and literal tear of all those inserted syringes over the years. He said it could have been dormant beneath the surface from some rude dope done maybe a year ago, and only recently did it fester to the surface with a vengeance. He said that it will open itself soon, so there is no need to lance it. That's what he said. Now it's two months later, and it's bigger and it won't open, no matter how many hot compresses he recommends. It just leaks this vile green shit from a tiny hole in the bottom corner. It's always a bitch, but tonight it outdid itself.

I go to the movies on 8th Street with my friend Ruth. It's getting chilly out, so I'm pretty heavily bundled. Once we take our seats, however, the temperature in the theater is somewhere around 120 degrees. So everyone is peeling off layers of clothing, including Ruth and I, but the last layer for me is this tight, long-sleeved sweatshirt. I sweat like I'm building pyramids while I watch the flick. It's one of those French soft-porn jobs, with enough platitudes in the dialogue to play the art-house circuit, and enough vaseline on the lens to lubricate every *gendarme* on the Champs

Elysées. The heat is so excruciating that getting turned on by these glib frog images is out of the question, but Ruth's hand is on my dick like it's a box of Raisinets.

It was all a total ordeal, and when the old "Fin" flashed on the screen, I let out a tiny yelp like a mutt given a bone.

I didn't load my clothes back on there at the seat, but carried them to the lobby. Standing right in everybody's path, I was about to pull on the first of two sweaters when I felt something liquid, and rather unpleasant, on my arm, beneath the sweatshirt. It wasn't sweat . . . this had a different texture. As people exited past us, I rolled up my sleeve to check out what the trouble might be, Ruth peering over my shoulder wondering what was holding me up. As I folded the tight, black fabric above my elbow, a monstrous, green substance, thick as rope, issued forth from the abscess like projectile vomit from the tiny mouth of an infant. It must have traveled a good three or four feet across the lobby, clinging to anything in its path: fur collars, suede handbags, chic tortoiseshell eyeglasses. None were spared . . . many were zapped. Those who weren't directly hit had to deal with the chain-reactive puking which was taking place among some weak-stomached onlookers. Many ran to the curb out on 8th Street and bent over, clutching parking meters for support. Some couldn't make it . . . watch out, alligator shoes! For her part, Ruth was in some lyrical dance of hysterics, somewhat Native American in its manner. She seemed to be feeding on the delusion that I was an alien being. Everything happened so quick . . . I thought it was sort of *funny* at first. Then I realized the crowd was getting genuinely ugly: "By God, the boy is an alien . . . let's kill him. *Kill him, I say!*" I ran off, knocking over a blind folk duet (guitar and autoharp), escaping finally down the mews off MacDougal Street.

When I got home, I examined the culprit on my arm. It seemed to have a mind of its own, I thought . . . and rather simpatico with my own, at that. To my regret, however, the little bugger was still intact. All that had happened was that the tight sweatshirt's sleeves, and the inordinate heat, had acted as a kind of two-hour compress throughout the movie, loosening the scum and puss beneath the wound to launch-ready consistency. The slow pressure of unrolling the sleeve squeezed it all to a point of frenzy by which it took flight. The hole at the bottom had enlarged somewhat, but otherwise, the tough flesh covering it was intact.

When I was a kid I imagined that I would one day inherit great, magical powers. Great strength, perhaps, or the ability to fly. As the years passed, these dreams drew limits on themselves, until they disappeared entirely. Now I realize there is a power I possess which others neither have nor comprehend. I myself witnessed its awesome display tonight in the theater lobby, and I was as overwhelmed as the others. It's not exactly the properties of power that I had fantasized about in my youth, but these things are mysterious in their ways.

THE DECISION TO LEAVE

I went to the strange church today . . . there's a major decision to be made. I have a chance to do a poetry reading out in California next week. That means free airfare out there and back, but if I want to stay out there, they tell me they'll just get a one-way ticket and add the money saved onto my fee. Since my friends out there have been harping so much lately in their letters and phone calls about the splendors of life on the West Coast, and since I need to make *some* kind of change, I may take up this offer. It's strange how it came right as I was thinking of this very move. It would be a radical switch, for sure.

I light a candle to St. Francis. I'm tired of these obscure, bottom-rung saints. I need a top-of-the-line saint to deal with this question.

One thing's certain: I have burned down this city in my flesh, heart and spirit. I've become so weary of New York's

speed, the ever-accelerating and forced perversity and vac-
illation. I'm sick of the need to *take it all in* . . . every party,
every opening . . . constantly tearing my body, almost literally, in different directions. I feel like some officer or,
more likely, some foot soldier who is fighting a war on four
fronts and always waiting for the transmission that he has
been invaded from yet another side.

I don't know how to undo what's been done. There is
an untraceable knot in my head of false facades I have set
up . . . dummy corporations whose addresses lead to no
place but a mail-drop in some abandoned storefront, the
windows blanked in whitewash.

There's no cool left in me. The only resources I retain
are a minimum of rage and controlled madness, barely
enough to offset the bullshit paraphernalia of art and the
city.

I don't know, maybe I should have stayed in college.
Now there's a fixed bet! Four years of a scrupulously washed
cunt sitting on your face.

I can't keep a steady style in my writing standing on
these shifting platforms of artifice and quick change. I try
to fuse my life and my work, to keep up with the tiresome
dodging of cars and drugs. But when you are walking such
a thin wire above such a chic and sleazy cosmopolitan abyss,
you don't stop to think. You *can't* stop. You just keep on
walking, your feet bent on the wire, intuition as your only
balance. Lately, balance is my job. I'm consumed by it. But
how long is the wire?

I know you may think this all somewhat histrionic, or
perhaps out-of-hand pretense. But here . . . I'm extending
my wrist to you . . . feel the pulse. Feel it.

I'm sick of writing about dope, about drugs in every
form. I'm sick of recording the ups of indulgence, and sick
of releasing dispatches of misery via abstinence. I thought
I could deal with, perhaps even come to understand, my
obsessions through some strained eloquence. I thought I
could eventually pierce every veil through chance meta-

phor, but how many flowers can serve as metaphors for that initial mingling of blood and water encased in the barrel of a syringe? All the Laotian roses . . . the Mariposa lilies, and now the hideous methadone I drink each morning, the color of a clown's orange fright-wig.

One thing's for sure, this stuff is no solution. They put you at the highest dose and figure that at least everyone's color television is safe from theft, but you're strung out worse than ever . . . only now it's sanctioned by the state. You're better off shooting junk, kids.

The fact is that instead of freeing myself through language, the language itself has become a hostage, and the room where we are held becomes smaller every day. The language needs room to maneuver. Only without boundaries can the words transform into something beyond themselves.

With all this in mind, I think I have come to a conclusion. I'll call and tell them I'm on my way. Bless you, St. Francis, and I would appreciate if you would extend me the same courtesy. I'll need it! For God's sake . . . California.

THE
MOVE
TO
CALIFORNIA

FIRST DAY IN CALIFORNIA

I touched down in California this afternoon. I need this place, this small town where I plan to take up residence. I need a disciplined landscape and the opportunity to respect the commonplace joys. I think I'm ready. I believe I have finally exhausted my New York City energies. I no longer live with obsessions that pull constantly in half a dozen directions. I'm ready for some precise boredom to wash over me, instigating a life where the choices are mine. I want to write in a room whose view doesn't change from day to day. A ravine with a eucalyptus grove holding my house in a brace of shadows, perhaps. I've been told by my poet friends who live here that eucalyptus thrives in this town . . . "When it rains it smells like coughdrops," Bill wrote me. I'm ready; I've had enough external stimuli, enough experience, courtesy of New York City, to last a hundred years. The certainty of my logic is the only thing that's truly frightening.

Susan met me in the terminal, and after sorting out my baggage, we were off toward the coast in her red Toyota, which, despite four open windows, smelled of stale vomit. "It was some asshole I met in the town bar last night," she explained. "He pissed in his pants, as well . . . I think in the same seat you are presently occupying." I slipped my *Times* beneath me, covering the violated seat. "The price you pay for bucket seats," I tossed back. "I sort of like the puke scent, though. It carries me right back to the city. I'll just shut my eyes and imagine I'm taking the "A" train straight to Bo Diddleyville, or whatever the name of this burg is."

"It's called Bolinas," she replied, lowering her voice to an almost reverent tone. "It's an Indian name for 'whale.' They used to mate in the lagoon there, until the white man logged the mountain beside it and let the silt wash into the water until it was too shallow. It's great there. You'll like it, though it may take a while . . . especially for *you*. What was it, that line you wrote referring to California?"

"The mecca of Clorox," I replied, my voice trailing off as my attention was suddenly pulled out the window, onto the hills we were passing. It was a community called Daly City, a sort of West Coast Levittown. The slopes were filled with uniform rows of tract houses, each home indistinguishable from the others. It wasn't just the dimensions and the architecture, however. All the homes seemed to have the exact same curtains, the same yard furnishings, the same flowers growing from the same green flowerbeds on the same yellow-trimmed casement sills. There was something else, too. Something that really put the chill on me. The clothes, the towels, the sheets hanging on lines in each back yard, had a kind of transcendent cleanliness. Surely, it was a brilliance unimaginable to one who every Monday as a child retrieved the family laundry drying on the tar rooftops of New York. It seemed to absorb sunlight. It was a mutant cleanliness, and it was a bit frightening. What was more horrifying were the shadows these mutated white sheets cast down across the hillside, where the grass was trim as a putting green. These shadows were counterpoint to the brilliant clean in their effect, darker by the same degree. I had never seen such pure black, ominous shadows.

My body suddenly felt damp. Was this some foreboding? I let it go, turning my attention back to Sue's flowing anecdotes about the splendors of bucolic living. One's senses are always sharpened on arrival, I figured. That would explain the phenomenon of West Coast light and shadow. I think it's healthy to be bent out of shape so abruptly on one's first day in a new place. Just as I was preparing myself patiently to indulge in the joys of the commonplace, an element of the strange sent a wave across the still pond.

Now the logic of my move has lost some of its certainty, and I'm less afraid for what is yet to come.

RESTLESS

I suppose moving to this little town, which has some form of beauty and wonder that transcends place (and time . . . most folks in this town are convinced the sixties never ended . . . they clutch that notion like an axe, and it's not smart to get within range while offering any dissenting opinions), and the fact that the majority of the people I spend any serious time with are old friends from Alphabet City on the Lower East Side, combine to blur comparisons of any sort between East or West Coasts. But as I withdraw more, cutting down on visits and spending the day walking long distances with my dog Jo'mama, sticking to a disciplined schedule of work and smoking dope and watching TV (which *is* better out here) at night, I began noticing again, in different manifestations, those perverse qualities of light and shadow.

The first thing I came to realize during those long treks along the coast through miles of bird sanctuary leading to the town of Point Reyes, or inland, up Mount Tamalpais (The Mountain of the Sleeping Maiden, a sacred place to its native inhabitants), is the fact that there is no real sense of history out here. In New England, you can't walk along any back road for long without spotting some plaque on a tree marking the very limb where some poor son of a bitch patriot was strung up by the Redcoats during the big one for independence. And not only were they hanged, they were, to the last, articulate as hell. Each plaque for each corpse riding the rope is sure to contain some witty slogan uttered just before the fatal moment. On my father's vacations, when I was just a tyke, we used to drive up along the backwoods surrounding Bear Mountain and West Point. There must have been three or four plaques to the mile (about the same number, I later realized, of bars to a single block in my uptown neighborhood). I always wondered, as we solemnly exited the car and shimmied up close to read the inscription, including those memorable last words, how all these guys managed to get caught if they were so clever. I was tempted to think they just might have been snagged because they were running in a direction opposite that of their fellow troops. Perish the thought . . . and, besides, that's not the point. What I'm saying is that, bogus epitaphs aside, there was a weight, an actual weight one could feel in those places. It was a sense of attachment . . . to what, I am not sure. Europe, I suppose. But that land seemed nurtured. I realize that the nurturing was, in large measure, in the form of spilled blood. Nothing unique in that, however. All I know is, to one child, the ghosts in those woods seemed content.

Not taking into account the formidable past of the Native Americans, I come up nil when it comes to any sense of history along my daily route, or the rest of this coast, for that matter. The weight is not here, and the ghosts are unsettled and restless. I mean, think about the recorded histories out here. The highlight seems to be butchering Indians (certainly the East was not immune to this) and rushing for gold in good old '49. Shit, these were events born of the same qualities possessed by their descendants in Orange County today, the same taught at front-line universities here (if you need an example, Stanford will do). The main quality is greed, and the arrogance and intolerance that come with it. I'm still amazed at the outright snobbery laid on me by those infected with this pioneer spirit. The minute they pick up on my New York accent (which is one badge I'll never surrender), I might as well be a nigger in Mississippi, circa '55, jumping some white man's place in line for the drinking fountain. The ghosts here are not content at all.

THE TAIL OF TWO CITIES

I spent my first day alone in San Francisco today, just walking around, digging the streets. They say this place has "charm" and "sophistication," but the latter is one of those words that always seems to bend when I try to nail it down. As for "charm," I suppose that means that the local purveyors of the strange-in-public are not only tolerated, but barely noticed. Take for example this man I saw today in a Chinese restaurant. He had a parrot on his shoulder that sang a medley of Donovan songs: *They call me Mellow Yellow . . . squawk!*"

I suppose the greatest distinction between New York and San Francisco (aside from the outrageous realization that you cannot buy pizza by the slice here) has to do with murder. They always find cute names for common serial killers here. Currently, there's the Zebra Killer who kills only whites, and the Zodiac Killer, who only kills when certain constellations dictate that the time is right.

That's the least of it, however. News editors anywhere dive into horrible shit and emerge with a catalog tag. Here (and I suppose I mean the West Coast in general on this), the very *means* of murder make the greatest difference. You see, in New York people pretty much take a gun and shoot somebody, or take a knife and stab someone. It's a fairly uncomplex procedure. Someone's dog shits on your Cadillac's whitewalls, and "Bang!" People gather, and the cops move them back: "Come on, nothin' to see folks." The TV crews interview the victim's neighbors: "He was a good man, a good husband and a good father. I never liked the dog myself." TV crews interview the killer's neighbors: "He was a quiet man; he preferred keeping to himself. But he seemed like a nice enough guy. He was a good husband and a good father. He always got on with my dog, though in general I don't think he liked them."

It's simple. It's routine. It's bland . . . rather democratic. The constellations play very little if any part in the murders in New York City. Out here in the bizarro city by the bay, things are different. A single bullet or a thrust of the knife does not suffice on the West Coast. More often, it seems, some poor fool is snatched into the back of a limousine by three men and a woman in black gowns with hoods. The guy, no doubt an innocent stranger, is taken to some cave along the ocean, encircled by a group of like-hooded ex-stock brokers and chefs of nouvelle cuisine, who chant obscenities in the Gregorian style. Then the guy is ceremoniously run through with an Egyptian dagger, castrated, diced into bite-size pieces and boiled in a cauldron of Crisco.

But perhaps I am nit-picking. In this century, such things are the by-products of "charm" and "sophistication" within such provincial borders. Anyway, after a stroll through Chinatown and a hasty homage to the beatnik quarters of North Beach, I'm on the bus home. The city, east or west . . . frantic or quaint . . . no longer owns me. I'm giving my time to the country life, living in the protective shadow of a sacred mountain.

THE VANISHING NUDE

Cassandra spent the entire night with me here, and her head was still beside me when I woke. That is a strange anomaly for the two of us. You see, there are only two constants in our relationship: we usually, since that first time on the beach, have sex outdoors, and she invariably, and often mysteriously, leaves me almost immediately afterward. I don't think I mentioned that time a few weeks ago, in a small meadow near the base of Mount Tamalpais, when in the middle of our post-coital embrace, she whispered that she had to take a piss. She stood, stretched her lovely naked body in the sun, which sprayed through the line of redwoods higher up the mountain, and went off to take care of business behind some bushes. I lay there waiting, smoking a joint and a cigarette in alternating drags, in extreme peace of mind. After a while, oblivious to real time, I realized that she was, by any clock, taking too long. I went over to the bushes. There was no trace of her, not even a wet spot on the floor of the pressed eucalyptus leaves. I yelled, but the only effect that had was scattering some swallows from the trees. I poked around another ten minutes or so, then decided that this case was closed.

Have I made clear the fact that she did not take her clothes into the bushes, that they were still there on the ground where we had lain? I picked them up and stuffed them in a bundle under my arm. Then I realized I was still totally naked myself, so I put the bundle down and got dressed. I'm not used to smoking grass in the daytime. I use it most evenings as a Pavlovian reward for keeping to my writing schedule that day. The sunlight was apparently increasing its effect many-fold. Having dressed, I picked up the bundle of Cass's clothing again and walked home.

It was at least a half-hour's walk, and I wondered all the way how she could make it back stark naked. She wouldn't mind if people saw her, at least not out of any sense of modesty. She would resent being seen for other, more complex reasons. She didn't like the people of this town. In her mind, *they* were the ones that caused her to be sent to that hideous institution. Her nude self would be a gift to those who saw it, and it was not the kind of gift she wanted to give these folks.

When I saw her the next day, downtown, outside the greasy-spoon breakfast joint, she just smiled. I asked her what happened; she just said she felt like leaving, explaining nothing more. She just smiled, and in that smile, more and more each time she flashed it, there was another hint of madness returning. Every time she pursed her gorgeous lips in that smile, she was taking another step back to that section of that hospital she had left behind, just a little less than a year ago.

So the mystery of the vanishing nude on the Mountain of the Sacred Indian Maiden (which just begs for a screenwriter) was never solved. And tonight when she stopped by, she seemed better. She was outright lucid, and the first thing out of her mouth, for perhaps the only time since I've known her, was not an inquiry into the whereabouts of the dope. We watched TV for half an hour, then retired to the bedroom. It really was quite odd, fucking indoors. Actually, the novelty of *a bed* seemed as strange and stimulating a piece of sexual paraphernalia as convex mirrors, handcuffs or a trampoline. With that the case, the night went on just swimmingly, so to speak. And again, I was not astounded when, instead of leaping out the window when we were through, she just laid her head on my shoulder and fell asleep, breathing so generously. I watched her a while before I fell out myself.

So, as I mentioned when I began this entry, she was still there beside me when I woke. She had swung over a bit to her own pillow. I was, as always, positioned exactly as I had fallen asleep. I should make this clear, because it's important that you know: You see, ever since I began using narcotics, I have slept in the exact same way. I lay on my back, my legs pressed together, and my arms folded across my chest with my hands pressed flat there. It is exactly like those tombs of crusaders that I've seen at the Cloisters in New York, and other museums: with the slab on top carved out as a life-sized effigy of the buried man. They are always laid to rest in that same position. Come to think about it, it's the same way Dracula lies in his coffin during the day . . . arms folded exactly like that on my chest. The hands pressed to each collarbone. The only difference is the tuxedo. And once set in said position, I never move when I sleep. I know all sorts of studies contradict this, and that scientists in this field *insist* that all people change their sleeping postures. They move a lot, in fact, and there is even some random order and significance to these movements, especially during periods of dreaming. But I still insist, and I've got witnesses: unless I am shoved by some exterior force (like a woman who wants to cop my blanket) *I do not move when I sleep*. And today, as always, I woke in that same position, Cassandra beside me.

I made coffee for both of us. By the time I was about to bring it into the bedroom, she was on the living room sofa wearing one of my oversized T-shirts. We drank the coffee and she told me something strange: "You know that thing, that hole in your arm that leaks the green shit . . . well, while you sleep, you caress it . . . you raise up both your arms and you take the left hand and, while you hold the right one straight up, you run your fingers over the hole. You do it in this way that's not only sensual . . . it's more than that. It's more than sexual, too. It's almost ritualistic . . . it's religious. Yeah, that's exactly it . . . it's like some religious ritual. And it's quite beautiful, the way your arms move. It's like a slow dance."

I was shocked, sitting there gaping. It wasn't so much what she said as the fact that she said it. Cassandra had never said so much in one outburst, and she *never* analyzed anything. Yet here she was with this lucid, incisive statement. And I didn't dismiss it as her schizoid dreaming either. Someone had made mention of the same thing once before. It was right when that abscess, the "hole in my arm leaking green shit" as Cassandra put it, first appeared. That was about six months ago. I've previously mentioned my rather gross obsession with it, so it would make sense that I'd allow it entrance into the already cluttered and abject landscape of my sleep. But to caress it? With a "religious" intensity? She made it sound like I was *sanctifying* this oozing pit, this cavern created by the abusive entrance of syringe points and the narco-garbage within them, whacked with only God knows what form of cutting agent . . . from powdered sugar to Italian baby laxative. Though it's only, in fact, about a quarter-inch in diameter, in my mind that hole is sometimes large enough to insert my own head, my whole body. I could climb in and see my past transgressions among the slime, or, if I have been doing this routine

Cassandra describes, perhaps I can put my lips to it and drink from it like a chalice. But will this act purify, or just further the decay? I've tried to open the thing, but the skin is too stubborn, hardened by the abuse into scar tissue. It just leaks. And now, it seems I've made it a ritual of my sleep.

I turn to Cassandra after dazing off within this rumination. She's not there. Her coffee cup is still full on the table, but she's gone. I hadn't heard a sound, what with my head stuck so deeply in that wound.

EXTRACTIONS

I woke this morning with a throbbing jaw and my right cheek inflated like a hard-on. It was painfully obvious that I had put off visiting a dentist long enough. I had to go over to the methadone program in San Rafael anyway, so I figured I'd get the name of a decent oral surgeon there and get it over with. If I had taken action when the pain began, some two months ago, I might have been able to have the tooth saved; but at this point there was no question about it . . . the sucker had abscessed and it would have to be yanked. This prospect produced mixed emotions. My last visit to a dentist was sort of blissful, actually. But that was two years ago.

Obviously, I'm one of those types who eschew the six-month check-up plan and make dental visits only when pain makes them essential, and the tooth itself has to go. It is for this reason that I never see the same dentist twice. This way I avoid those hideous oral hygiene lectures they thrive on giving you while they've got you captive at a 140-degree angle spitting out vile-looking shit into a device resembling a minature toilet bowl, inches from your face. If they haven't seen you before, you can always put up some bullshit story about how you were stuck up in the Arctic Circle, working at a research station monitoring the solar winds. "It was terrible, Doc. There was some snafu with the supply plane . . . they parachuted us three-hundred cases of chocolate bars . . . it was all we had to survive . . . another time it was pralines . . ."

So I've already dropped two wisdom teeth. The last one was at that visit two years back, and it was, indeed, a strangely pleasant experience. I asked around the drug circuit where I could find a competent guy who had no aversion to doling out a steady stream of nitrous oxide, along with any other pain reduction technique available to the bold new medical frontier. The guy I was eventually steered to was all that and more. He had a thriving practice in Spanish Harlem and, though he had a bunch of capable nurses floating about, he was the only dentist in a huge room with eight surgical chairs. All eight were constantly filled by a rotation of vociferous Puerto Ricans, and he moved from chair to chair with incredible speed and finesse, instructing the nurses on what to do to prep each patient. Then he would step in and take care of the main business, finishing the semi-supine casualties off with amazing speed. He was good, too. The whole thing reminded me of one of those spooky whiz-kid chess players who carry on simultaneous games with a dozen or so opponents, and wind up kicking ass all around in a bone-like minimum of moves.

"So how are we doing?" He approached me, the nurse handing him my X rays.

"It's the one back here," I pointed, "hurts like a mo . . ."

"Oh, I see . . .yeah," he cut me off, "Yep. Gotta come out. I *could* try to save it. You want me to try? You don't? Okay. Listen, I'm going to give you some of this gas here . . . (a nurse attached the mask) . . . I think you'll enjoy this. It will make you feel sort of giggly. The music sounds nice on it . . . that's Tito Puente, but I got Hendrix coming up. You listen to the music and relax. I'll be back in about twenty minutes."

It was amazing. Twenty fucking minutes of frozen brain. I was in Heaven.

Actually, I was in Central Park. In my mind, that is. It

was fall and these beautiful leaves were blowing in my face. I was walking across the Sheep Meadow, but instead of grass growing out of the ground, there were millions of bottles, very tiny bottles, of codeine cough medicine. I slid across them until I reached a slight incline, then I went rolling down, building up speed, pushing wind-blown leaves and copies of *The New York Times* out of my way so that I could see. Then the scene switched. I was at some amusement park. It could have been anywhere. I was in a bikini swimsuit going down one of those long, winding water slides, buoyed up on thin jets of blue water. Right in front of me was Elvis Presley. It seemed I was moving faster than him because I sort of straddled around him, my fingers pinching his nipples, my lips hanging on his ears. He yelled out over the considerable noise, utilizing the full projection of his twangy voice, that this was a mistake and that he was not "the one." I asked him who "the one" was, and he instructed me: "Son, all you have to do is turn around."

I was moving mighty fast, so it was all I could do to make a turn. But I made it, a full 180 degrees. From my new vantage point, I saw what was behind me all along. It was a beautifully radiant woman/child, no more than five feet away. We were both sliding down that endless chute at equal velocities, so the distance between us remained the same. She couldn't speed up, and I couldn't slow down. We could only look into each other's eyes, which were clear and wide from the acceleration. I was reading deep secrets inside those eyes when I heard a strange masculine voice (and it definitely wasn't Elvis) say, "Damn, I think I broke it in half!"

I suddenly stopped dead on the chute, my cock was hard and had weaseled its way out of my bikini. The girl sped right at me, completely naked and legs spread wide. "This is going to be incredible," I said to myself.

But just as she was about to mount me at untold velocity, I heard that same strange man saying, "Okay, good. I've got it. That's it. We're all done." Meanwhile, the gas mask was yanked from my face, and my nitrous oxide-fueled fantasy was replaced by the harsh image of bright lights and the dentist smiling down at me.

"Have a good time?" he asked.

"Never felt a thing, Doc," I answered, then added cryptically, "and unfortunately, neither did she."

As for the joker I was steered to today, he was brutal. He refused to give me the good old gas, or anything for that matter, except simple injections of novocaine. He also had a touch like some master out of a chamber of horrors. I didn't care at this point, knowing that the transcendental pain I was dealing with now would finally put an end to the unyielding torture I had had to endure daily.

He was fast; I'll say that much for him. The whole thing was over within ten minutes, including the time it took him to write out a prescription for Percodan. I filled it at a pharmacy, swallowed an excessive amount, and hitchhiked home. I had the tooth, eaten deep and brown by decay, in my pocket. The dentist thought it odd that I would want such a souvenir, but he relented when I told him that I intended to show it to my son as an "object lesson."

After I got back to the house, I greeted the mutt and took him for a long walk on the beach. I felt great. There was a dull soreness in my jaw from the extraction, but that obscene, pulsating ache was gone. I took the tooth from my pocket and held it up against the background of the ocean. I thought how strange it was that such a tiny object could be the source of a pain that seemed to encompass my entire universe for a time. When I had that ache and looked at a tree, then the tree itself seemed to be suffering. It also seemed odd that one could purge this misery with so simple an operation. If only all our pains could be so easily remedied, I thought. I flung the tooth as far as I could into the rushing tide, letting it sink to the bottom and never return.

DURING THE STORM

First I hear the pounding of horses' hooves. They are moving from the far slope of the hill across the street to the side visible from my window. They gallop in complete unison, so the sound is like an organ key jammed down, producing a single, long drone. It's strange, because they never move to this side of the hill until evening, and it's barely four P.M. In the city you learn to deal with constant, petty anomalies, but here in the country, I have come to know that nature does not deal out variations without large and often mean consequences.

So I'm not totally surprised when I hear the first distant thunder, and see the first banks of clouds, black and quick, roll over the top of the mountain. Then the lightning. I settle against the back of the sofa, a blanket wrapped around me. I get up and split a small log on the slab beside the wood stove and throw it in. I don't need so much heat, but it makes me feel prepared. When I feel prepared, I feel lost. When I feel lost, I feel comfortable.

The lightning produces incredible shapes against the sky's black canvas . . . bent daggers . . . collapsing stairways. There is a single stallion right on the crest of the hill, its head raised regally. The pose reminds me of Roberto Clemente standing at home plate. Suddenly a bolt rises from behind him. It creates the effect of a focused fire spit from the stallion's wide mouth, as if he were playing a game with the elements, throwing it all back at the sky.

Since childhood I have loved the fear a storm brings. Inside that fear I feel alive. Inside that fear we are forced to transform knowledge to wisdom . . . all our learned trivia into principles.

The rain builds, comes now like sheets slung over a line. It is not that frantic or digressive rain; this is the sound of that certain rain, steady and dependable. It has an elegance which soothes the beast that has disseminated itself in particles of another liquid in my veins, so that an equilibrium is reached. It's as if a car you have driven in the night off some poorly marked bridge has at last filled up with water, just as you have given up fighting the pressure against the door, trying to escape. Now the pressure is equalized. The door opens and you swim to the surface, which is much nearer than you thought. You suddenly realize the great respect due nature and its laws.

I've never seen the sky this dark. Wait . . . there was a time. It was back in New York. I was very young and it was mid-afternoon of a Good Friday, near the hours when Christ hung on His cross. I remember old Irish ladies running in their housecoats into the church, their fingers already beginning the first decade on their rosary beads. I was with my mother. We had just gotten an orange drink at Nedick's. I was terrified. I broke away from her hand holding mine and ran across the street into the church, my mother chasing after me. She was furious because it was the first time I had crossed a street by myself. In the church I knelt and mumbled under my breath, *"Glory be to the Father, the Son and the Holy Ghost . . . as it was in the beginning, is now and ever shall be, world without end. Amen."*

There is something weird about the storms here. They seem to have a different shape than those back east. And you think of different things. Here I watch nature perform. In New York I watched people react. I'd watch pimps rolling up windows in their Cadillacs, shutting out their whores and signaling them back to work. Then they light a smoke and sink low into zebra skin upholstery, like insects surviving through camouflage with their natural environment.

In New York City, rain provides something of a social function. People gather in small spaces, in hallways and storefronts, and begin to talk. They speak in civilized tones which some of them had all but forgotten. They tell strangers things they would never think of revealing to friends or

lovers. During a storm in New York, people actually *agree*
with things you say.

Here in California, in northern California, you move
deeper and deeper inside your imagination as the storm
grows. You throw another small log on the fire, believing
the heat will preserve each image. I imagine the monarch
butterflies on the hill of Terrace Avenue scattering, millions of them, from their inverted grip on the eucalyptus
branches. Some find shelter in the denser pines, others are
struck directly while in their deep migratory suspension,
blasted by drops as wide as their sealed wings. They are
driven to the cracked pavement below. I picture myself
walking there tomorrow, when things are only half dried.
They'll be pressed tight, like small crescent leaves, across
the tar road, ready to be peeled off like postage stamps. I
conjure up an image of them flawlessly spelling out a name
there on the pavement: "Vladimir Nabokov."

When I was about eight years old, my parents rented a
bungalow upstate for the month of August. I remember
sitting out a hurricane there. Some of the guys from the
neighborhood were visiting us at the time; there was a huge
blaze in the old open fireplace. I think it was the only
occasion we ever needed to use it, aside from burning the
thick piles of newspaper each Sunday evening. There were
four of us playing a board game—I think it was *Clue*—and
we were each seated in an overstuffed armchair, sunk in
as deep as that pimp in his Caddy, riding out the storm.
The chairs' arms touched each other, forming a sealed,
safe square around the table holding the board. It seemed,
though we each felt an exquisite fear, that nothing could
penetrate the sanctuary of that square. The lights were
down; we played by candlelight. It was, perhaps, my only
true mystical experience. Of course we didn't understand
it, but we had wordlessly formed a design that was impen-
etrable to any elements, to any danger. God, I want to find
a chair that is large enough to make me young again . . .
young enough to begin constructing that square again.

LOW EBB

I seem to have reached a low ebb, and there's no mistaking the cause. It's this hideous methadone, which has turned my life into something like bad surrealism, i.e., no surprises or revelations, just a feeling of lethargy. Every morning I wake and down my dosage, drink coffee and wait for it to take effect. When it does hit, the euphoria of those earlier days is gone. I lie in bed, prey to a compulsion for neatness. I line up books to read that I seldom touch, and notebooks I open and shut, entering nothing but, perhaps, a drawing of a stick figure beneath a cloud, or single words, like, "abbatoir" or "serpentine mist," I lay out neatly three brands of smokes in separate rows. The main decision each morning is choosing which brand to light up next. And I smoke incessantly. One after the other. It's obscene.

What makes it worse is what's right outside the door. This is no tenement on Avenue B. I'm on my back in a filthy room two blocks from the ocean. There's a tree dropping overripe plums right outside the window, as if in homage to my own decay. Shit, William Carlos Williams *stole* all those goddamn plums from his good friend's ice box, and here I am unable to pick them fresh and delicious before they fall dead in my yard.

My dog comes bursting in, wet with the ocean, licking salt from between his paws. He looks at me like, "Come on . . . what the fuck is up? You should feel the energy of those waves. Look, here's a new tennis ball I just found. Let's go to that clearing on the mesa. You throw; I fetch . . . hey, it will be fucking great!" I get up and dressed. He's right. I'm going to start using my time.

LYING WITH THE DOG

My dog sleeps with me. It's nice. He lies always in the same spot, at the bottom of the bed, with his little head on my right ankle. When the weather turns cold, he simply comes up and climbs beneath the covers and pads his way to the exact same place, resting his head. Only then can I feel his fuzzy neck and chin. I've come to rely on these simple pleasures.

Last night I had a hideous nightmare. Usually I can guide my dreams once they arise, bad or good. But there is no control when the dream takes place in the room where I'm actually sleeping. No guiding the horror of the man standing in the corner, or emerging from the closet with luminous eyes, holding a huge syringe-like scepter, advancing at me, speaking in tongues. ("*Tubalar,*" he says, that's the only word I can remember, "*Tubalar.*")

Then I can't separate the dream; can't divide it from the reality of my room. I've begun a program of detoxification, and the lower my dose of mojo juice, the more often this person invades the one sanctuary where I cannot ward off the nightmare's cunning, or control the demons. He comes in various costumes; he knows the rituals of my vulnerabilities.

But last night, as always when it happens, when I wake up drenched in toxic sweat, sometimes screaming, Jo'mama comes up to my face and licks, and kneels there like a sentinel. I'm open to such gushing sentiment. I welcome it. I've suppressed it too long. I thank God for the dog . . . he calms me down, and that's as much as you can ask for. It surely is enough to feel free to lick him in return, before I can risk more sleep, and he goes back to my ankle and yawns as he circles once before he rests his head there.

IMPAIRED

It's been awhile since I have written. That's because I made a large—perhaps too large—leap downward on my methadone dosage about two months ago, and it is only now that I've stabilized enough to write. Physically, I'm not too bad. I sneezed once every twenty seconds or so the first four days, and that was most unpleasant, but I'm holding on.

My brain feels detached . . . literally, that is, as if the liquid that suspends it evenly inside my head, like those marine compasses . . . I'm sure you've seen them . . . well, it's as if that fluid were drained off and the corduroy-textured bulk of gray was loose, banging itself freely against the inner walls of my head, leaving chunks of itself there at times, shriveling and drying without the protection of the vital, viscous fluid which provides a sort of nurturing balance.

I'm not sure what the exact results of this are. Photophobia, for one . . . the light gives everything a sinister frame. I've never subscribed to that wank theory about people having "auras," but in sharp sunlight, everything looks cheetah-like . . . ready to pounce.

My dog is the loser; he gets shorter walks than usual. But since I can't get more than a cavity full of sleep (which reminds me: my teeth ache, individually and as one), I am able to go up to the meadow in the first light of dawn and indulge him in the splendors of tennis ball fetch. Being up at that hour, I invariably run into my friend, the poet Tom Clark, who actually jogs six miles a day (wearing one of those Superfly, Back-to-Africa pillbox jobs). He never stops. We seldom speak, but simply nod at each other with a look of camaraderie born of the knowledge that we have both succeeded in our quest to become complete anti-social hermits, dazzling and mysterious—at least to our pets—in our exquisite reclusion . . . although his reclusive condition is a bit healthier than mine at the moment.

I always get back before the sun rises to its first, somehow irritating, force. You'd think it would be the perfect time to create long poems out of my lustrous aching, but until this rather forced entry, I just didn't have the ability to recall that such things are what I'm supposed to do. That is, not only did I not give a shit, but I had no inkling that I was supposed to. Even now, I'm forcing it, and I suppose it's evident (which is alright as long as you understand that I'm *impaired*). But I came here to the West Coast to get steady . . . to shake the snake-like vacillations in my life. Stability. It just doesn't seem proper to be confused in California.

GETTING IT ALL BACK

I ended my entry abruptly yesterday. That was in some part because my endurance has faltered during my detox. Writers, like athletes, must get back in shape at a slow, steady pace. But that was not the main reason I cut myself loose.

The thing is, I'm still fighting back the heebie-jeebies from this drop in my dose of mojo juice. The words themselves seem strange from the moment they release themselves from my pen. It's as if there is a great distance between the tip of this writing instrument and the white field of the page, with its thin lines like lanes in a super-highway. It's as if, from that distance, which is more like an altitude, the words were parachuting down, subject to the whims of strange currents of air, so that, by the time they touch down and roll a bit, they are not in the place I expected them, nor do they land with the same meaning. I tried the typewriter but it was as bad, or worse. Each letter typed seemed to chew up the one before it like a vicious dog so that no words could be completed. If I did compile enough words to complete a phrase, they eventually would disassemble from their linear path like parked cars filmed in stop action over the course of an entire day.

It's all as if words, phrases, images, syntax were small glass beads from a necklace which was wrenched from some neck and spilled on the floor and down the sides of sofa cushions and armchairs and under bookshelves and maybe swallowed by the cat. I've got to find *all* the glass pieces before I can even reorder the color sequence, and restring it and tie it tighter than before. There's always a splendor in beginning all over. Even if it means getting on one's knees to search beneath that bookshelf or prospecting through years of lint and ashes beneath those cushions. Even if it means breaking open that cat's shit, which it conveniently has deposited in a plastic box, more orderly than any secretary could ever hope to be.

Then I'll appreciate the value of each bead—rather, each word and image—that much more, never wasting another. And I will, I swear to myself, get it all back in time, string it all together, tighter, as I said, than before.

THE BABYLON WHEEL

A dream last night. Not a pleasant one, but since I've undertaken my detox, I've gotten little sleep each night, and any dream is a welcome diversion.

I was walking through an amusement park, a gray, chilled dawn. It was not abandoned; everything was functional and clean. The cars of the roller coaster shone in the thin drizzle as if dew-covered. It was more like a day off: closed, unattended. Even the landscape beyond the park's fence seemed closed. The canary-yellow tract houses on the slope, the fog rising off bitter lawns, unattended. A day off, as well, for the more distant mountain. Atrophy, and the fear of it, breeds. I heard the sound of unoiled pulleys and slashing metal and walked slowly toward it . . . if it hadn't been a dream, I would have walked much faster.

Just around a large quonset hut, I saw it. The angle I had was so dead-on straight that it seemed one-dimensional at first. I moved right for a better view. It was the largest ferris wheel I had ever seen. It made the ones at, say, Rye Beach or Coney Island seem a child's Erector Set in comparison. Not as elaborate as Ezekiel's Wheel, but worthy of its name, "The Babylon Wheel," spelled out in flashing variegated lights, shaped as a rainbow above the ticket booth. I approached the man in the booth. He resembled a ventriloquist's dummy (something I've always feared), the rouge thick on his cheeks, the evanescent gaze. He handed me a ticket and bent over as if he were considerately folding himself in half for someone to carry away. I entered through a turnstile, a man from nowhere sliding suddenly up beside me. "You needn't have bothered to pay," he whispered. The words appeared to arrive too late for the movement of his lips, as if they were coming from somewhere else, and they were purposefully out of synch.

I looked up at the wheel. Each car—and there were too many to count—was a giant human skull. You were lowered into the seats from above, like a surgeon's probe, so that once seated you were contained completely within, your only means of seeing out onto the landscape—which is pretty much the point on any ferris wheel—was through the cavities of the eyes, each the size of the windshield of an eighteen-wheeler.

Making a dream leap in time, I found myself inside one of the skulls, moving upward. There were pools of ectoplasm-like stuff glistening on the floor, and patches of flesh in their final stage of decomposing on the inner walls, though the seats were of a fine velvet. I was obviously inside what was once the skull of a living being, albeit a very, very large one. The smell was strange; not really putrid, it was more like the blissful aroma of amyl nitrate. Another dream leap: the stranger was sitting next to me, wearing a thin robe, a jockstrap and thigh-high boots. He placed his arm around me. I knew who he was in the instant of his upward stare. He was, let's say, the owner of this ride . . . of the whole park, no doubt. Perhaps this dream?

He spoke in a language I couldn't understand, the same doppler effect, words badly lip-synched. The indistinguishable sentences made my cock erect. He undid his robe. The thing in his jockstrap was like some octopus tentacle, its tip writhing in the ectoplasm on the floor. I could feel the urgency, the anxious heat of being halfway through a wet dream, surge through my pipes like molten lead from the company's cauldron. His face twisted, became an erosion of spectacular, hideous flowers. He grabbed me, and in the dream my eyes focused on infinite shelves, rows of his own curios of evil, vile and delicate as a pederast's smile. His hand knew the way better than my own. I was just about there, then my impatient body jumped ahead of my mind.

Then I woke. I sat up and let it fold; there was no way I was going to consummate his faggot lust. That, I realized, is the great beauty of dreams: the devil may inevitably find a way to jerk you off, but you *can* always wake up before he makes you cum.

MATTERS LITERARY

God, I've gotten myself so straight I can actually think about matters of the literary sort.

For example, why did Kerouac wind up so concerned with (among so many other obsessions) his own lies? Deceit is an active, energetic (and energizing) pursuit. Naturally, I'm speaking about matters literary, not about old ladies, priests, or a blind man in traffic ("Don't worry yourself sir . . . no, of course the light *hasn't* changed yet, hee hee!"). I mean, I'm not some vile thing. But literature-wise, honesty is so horribly passive. It's also a sly tool for a facilitating reductionism . . . e.g. Hemingway. Though, that said, I *do* see, as well, how total honesty can be beautifully dream-like. And I don't mean to confuse that with "surrealism," which is like a girl next door whom I love so badly I must ignore.

TORN WEB

I've been clean from my last dose of methadone for about a week now, living on that ironic, acute high that invariably comes when you stop taking drugs. I may as well enjoy it. I know from experience just how short a time it lasts. Within three or four weeks the brilliance surrounding everything will fade like a cheap paint job, and the pace of boredom will gather it all back into its tedious grip.

For now I prepare myself, trying to rethread the needle and mend my frayed senses. Living in the country is an advantage; it's easier to decipher what's for real when the music's not too loud. I don't have to shuffle all over town hearing people at parties tell me how great it is that I'm straight and how good I look . . . until all their distorted voices, whether glib or sincere, send me up the wall, where the man is waiting.

I have to reregister a room for my heart. It's been waiting a long time, somewhere outside, without so much as a whisper of protest. That abandonment wasn't just an abuse, it was a sin.

Today I went for a long walk with my dog, up to Mount Tamalpais. I watched a pumpkin spider for hours, weaving its web across a tri-pronged branch on a dead thorn bush. After watching all the insect death and escape, and the repairs that followed, I wanted to feel the web. It was nothing more than tactile curiosity. I reached out and fingered a piece, but I couldn't control my newly recovered senses. The fine tuning of my touch was off. I just couldn't gauge the resilience of the web. I was too caught up in the vibrance of the orange hump on the spider, and the silver intricacy of the weave. By the time I pulled my hand free, the whole web was torn apart. It seems the deeper I allow my perceptions to penetrate, the more ruin I leave in my wake.

CHRISTMAS IN CALIFORNIA

Spending Christmas last week in California seemed a bit absurd, the climate and surroundings evoking none of my youthful remembrances. In a sense, that was a good thing . . . Christmas has given me nothing but a flair for inventive suicides since I passed the salad years of that holiday at the age of nine. Out here in the mecca of Clorox, the date just slid by with a surreal thievery. The smell of eucalyptus permeating these roads does not do much for me in the way of wintry nostalgia, except recollections of cough drops and seasonal colds and that frightful balm my mother would heat and rub on my chest while I was laid up in bed on the big day, while I heard my brother out in the living room running down the batteries on my toys, if not wrecking them outright.

Even the Nativity scene at the local church here seemed suspect. When I passed by I saw the straw in the manger under serious attack by these monstrous turkey buzzards, who had knocked flat two adoring shepherds and Joseph's donkey and whose truly enormous wingspans threatened to decapitate a wise man as they scattered at my approach.

There was one effect I had not bargained on and which I cannot explain, but without the trappings of snow, bogus Santas and fir trees in vacant lots being hawked for outrageous markups, I found myself thinking of it more as a holyday than a holiday, taking in Mass and, more importantly, not feeling a hypocrite for it. The rest of the day, as I recall, I spent the better part of three hours climbing two adjoining trees in the fault-line ravine to rescue one of my cats.

SHADOWBOXING

Since I detoxed from methadone, I've felt an almost magnetic impulse to return to New York. What's strange is that this comes at a time when I'm just beginning to enjoy my life here, to come to terms with the pace. I don't buy that shit about how New York City is the art center of the world, and you just got to be there if you want "it" (and I have no idea what this all-purpose "it" means, consists of, signifies, or uses for food and drink) to happen. Truth be known . . . I'd just as soon live on the far outskirts of that world, sending in a postcard now and then.

But still, this longing to return exists. I can't deny it. I have a suspicion the answer lies in the very resources I've gained in this place. I want to test the understanding and, well, *wisdom* that I've accumulated. I'm like a boxer making a comeback out in the sticks, where I was sent by too many knockouts in the big city. I've been lifting weights, sparring and doing miles and miles of roadwork. Now I've got to see if I can compete. Just compete. I don't want a shot at the title.

The problem is, I might be setting myself up for a blow that I can't walk away from. Some friends out here who I've consulted on this possible move think that might be the case. Worse still, they think I know it too, and that I want to walk into that blow. That self-destructive line wears thin, however. As far as my opposition goes, it's all just shadowboxing anyway, and it makes no difference where the wall is, nor the light you adjust behind you.

A SPECIAL DELIVERY

This morning I opened the front door to let out my dog and, with a sensation of fireflies fluttering through my spleen, I found the leg of a goat. I am not speaking here of a misplaced delivery from the butcher, all cleaned and sectioned, but the entire leg of a goat, freshly dissevered at the top of the thigh. It was covered with its thin layer of black hair, textured like the crewcut of a Marine drill sergeant. The blood where it had been cut off (by what seemed to be a serrated blade of some kind . . . perhaps a saw) was not that day-old hue similar to tincture of iodine, but a red as fresh and true as if you had just gotten a paper cut on this very page. It could not have been more than an hour old, two at the very most. But by far the worst part was the infamous cloven hoof, its groove filled with dark mud and all the Satanic mythology of a millennium. All the pages of my studies of the occult turned before me, and nothing within them could equal the horror of this thing at my feet.

I resorted to calm logic. My own dog was locked in, but

surely some other dog had left it there, having dragged it from one of the farms on the mesa. There are plenty of dogs that come pawing at my door, knowing I'm always good for a handout. That must be the answer. Then again, I am overlooking the fact that dogs are usually the pet emissaries of the dark one.

There are, as a matter of fact, some demon worshipers around this town, but they are strictly Ticketron satanists. They drop some peyote during the full moon and dance around a bonfire chanting gibberish, then sit and recite lines from pop songs. More Margaret Hamilton in *Oz* than Gille de Rais in his fortress.

Though I've always been fascinated with the occult, I don't know where I stand on it, so to speak. Sometimes I think we have, as a wasted bunch of beings, not yet earned the right to the occult. However, I believe that evil exists, and not as the symptom of mental disorder, but as a pervasive entity. The immediate question, of course, is whether this entity had any hand (or paw) in the special delivery at my doorstep. And, more worrisome still, if there happens to be some sort of postage due.

THE FAT BAT

Last night, just as I was getting over the incident of the goat leg, I woke up to Jo'mama barking and bouncing around the bed. I then heard a sound like someone rapidly turning the pages of a huge book. In the light of a bright crescent moon, I saw this large bat flapping around the room. Not only was its wingspan quite wide, but it was actually *fat*! "A fat bat!" I yelled out, though no one was around to hear. "Holy shit."

My first inclination was to dive under the sheets, and that is precisely what I did. From that vantage point, I realized I was going to have to take some action . . . open a window, run for the broom and chase it out.

I was not looking forward to this. My fear of bats is both

irrational and intense. The fact is, up until this moment, I had never seen a live bat. I remembered that old adage about them going for your hair and getting all tangled up in it, so I reorganized my plan to include the seizing of a hat off the hanger near the door.

I gave a peek out from the sheets. It was pandemonium. My two cats were now in the room, bouncing off the walls with outstretched claws trying to down the intruder. "Good cats," I cheered, "Get the fat bat." The bat itself was in a bit of a panic. It moved its wings almost mechanically, like one of those wind-up, polyurethane birds I had as a kid, made by the same company that came out with hula hoops and Frisbees. It was a horrid thing with a small rat-like head, paper-thin wings and a bloated belly which shone an iridescent purple in the moonlight. It totally lived up to my irrational fear. I dashed out from my cover and, in almost a single motion, grabbed a cap and put it on, then went into the living room, right outside my bedroom door, and snatched the broom. Waving the broom about like a crazed Russian peasant lady, I followed it, whacking a wing now and then. It was only after a full minute of this fool- ishness that I realized I had failed to open the window through which I would chase the bat out. Warding it off with the broom in one hand, I raised up the window with the other. Within a matter of seconds, the bat flew out. I watched it disappear into the eucalyptus grove, flying with infinitely more grace now that it had escaped these mad confines.

It was now 3:00 A.M., and I was wide awake, wearing a hat. First a goat's leg . . . now a bat . . . an extraordinarily fat bat, at that. I have never been one for superstition, I can pull the Grim Reaper from a Tarot deck and not blink, but when certain signs knock so loudly and insistently at my door, I listen. I had no idea how I was about to interpret these events, if they meant some minor demon wanted me out of town, or if they foreshadowed the big earthquake. I didn't know, or care.

Despite the hour, I dialed, then and there, the number of American Airlines. I'd been checking out the comparative prices for flights to New York for the last few weeks, knowing the move back there was inevitable, and American was cheapest last time I looked. I reached the artificial-sounding voice on the other end and booked a flight for this coming weekend. I can always cancel it, but I don't think I will. It is a risky proposition, this return, but, what with such exigent, concise indicators as a goat's leg and a fat bat, my choice is clear. Besides, I don't think that my demon's purpose is to get me out of this town, but more likely to get me back to New York City. I feel clean enough now not to back down.

BACK
TO
NEW
YORK

THE LAST MAN ON EARTH

Some days the loneliness of being back in New York, drug free but still not adjusted to it, transforms its frustration into a warm sensation, providing an energy which is perfectly parallel to the task, leaving no residue for anxiety, fear or rage. I imagine myself, then, the last man left on earth.

These are days that seldom come, and why and how they present themselves, from the very moment I wake, I have no idea. As you can imagine, I have sought to devise a formula to artificially initiate this feeling. I eat what I recall eating before the last one came, I read the same passages from the same books, I retire at the exact hour and minute as recorded in the log, but this chance euphoria cannot be induced. It is, apparently, a totally arbitrary phenomenon . . . a gift from the one god left who has not abandoned this crumb of life.

No matter. I accept this gift, and on those rare days when it comes I like nothing so much as to take inventory, slowly and effortlessly, as if I were wrapped in a deep quilt and dreaming it all beside a fire, oblivious to the endless winds of endless winters, to assess my stores with precision and fondness. It's strange how this act, which is nothing but a tedious chore any other day, becomes such a complete indulgence now. I sample bits of food with a keener taste, I glance over those same books, whose quick chapters take on a magical coherence and animation. My hands caress the pages. I make quick, clever drawings with my many colored pens.

But that is the very nature of this gift: a pure and even sense of timelessness. So I make a second cup of coffee to sip within the progress of my task, and I set about it.

HELLO DALI

Today, right in the glare of the sun bent by the giant facades of midtown, I was robbed of a cab by one of the world's most famous living artists. It's true . . . check this. I had just finished my monthly sojourn to the art galleries along 57th Street, and I was thinking about what dogs nearly all the exhibits were (I may not know what I like, but I know art, and these shows were truly canine). The one exception, which made this trip uptown worthwhile, was the Alex Katz exhibit. He had these giant paintings of orange flowers. The movement of the colors made you recoil as you entered the room, as if you'd fired a very high-caliber rifle. I suppose I was walking in my usual midtown daze . . . it seems whenever I venture above 14th Street and beneath 96th, I am struck by some partial epilepsy. I imagine it's a defense device against the shattering medleys of wealth and beautiful women. Whenever I return home from these trips, I find huge black and blue welts on my hips from walking into parking meters.

Actually, my defenses were, for the most part, failing me today. The weather was just turning mild after a particularly harsh winter, and the uptown women were taking the opportunity to shed their long coats and display those tight-monied asses in tight silk pants or chic blue jeans. It was devastating. Men's heads were turning with that urgency usually reserved for auto accidents. I try to avoid this crass leering, I really do; but then something walks by that simply will not stand still, so to speak, for any resistance. It's true, there is some perverse element in scoping ass of wealth and means that just does not exist with the penurious bottoms of one's own class, however fine.

But let me get back to my run-in with the famous artist. As I've already noted, I am quite willing to admit I may well have been somewhat in the grip of a midtown trance. But how bad could it have been? After all, I was out there on 57th between Fifth and Sixth avenues between two parked cars, flagging a cab with that arm-hand motion that says, "I grew up here, so give me a fucking break." You need to have sharp wits about you to get a cab in New York . . . any jerk knows that. And I did, in fact, get a cabbie's attention. There he was pulling right up to me, wedged in tight between two double-parked delivery trucks. The situation was clear: It was my cab.

Then things happened, fast and chaotic, yet smooth as the curve of a Henry Moore sculpture. This radically visible couple, each flailing their arms and chattering speedily in French, exited the building right in front of me. They were obviously coming from some art show, because it was one of those six-story buildings with nothing but galleries on every floor. I had my hand on the grip to the cab's door, but I couldn't take my eyes off this couple. They were both, despite the breakthrough of spring, wearing ankle-length sable coats. Those coats must have cost enough to bite a very large chunk off the deficit of last year's Soviet economy. Because of the wild French and the crazed Latin gesticulations, I had thought they were arguing furiously, but in any eye's shutter they were peering adoringly at each other, her furry arm linked in his. I noticed her first. That was natural . . . she was stunning, her hair dark and savage, full lips with cream gloss, and large brown eyes with lashes as long and sharp as daggers on a child's charm bracelet. Her coat was unbuttoned, flung open with severe purpose, revealing brown leather pants on long legs leading to Spanish boots. Above a waist adorned with a huge buckle that looked like actual tortoiseshell, she wore a thin cashmere sweater, its cream color matching her lipstick. God, was she fast with the moves. Within no more than two seconds, she had flung her hair back salaciously three and a half times, pursed, pouted and parted her lips four times, and fluttered those huge lashes uncountable times, faster than a hummingbird's wings when its beak's in the nectar. They were so thick with mascara that I believe I actually, over

the traffic horns and engines of trucks, heard them clicking . . . a timepiece with an overwound spring.

   This all occurred within a very small envelope of time,
you must understand. I was still holding the taxi door by
its handle, and had washed off enough dazzle from my
brain to push the button there and slightly open the door.
The cab driver made no complaints. He was in no big
hurry; he too had taken intense notice of this woman with
the audible eyelids. Several men around the immediate
area had also noticed, and several beyond. But my attention
had somehow been drawn to the man beside her, and it
was only an instant before the currents of recognition were
ignited. Nobody douched by celebrity could be more rec-
ognizable . . . the blue-black moustache, long and thin and
curled like a mandala to fame, the mischievous eyes literally
twinkling and the trademark silver cane inlaid with dark
gemstones. It was Salvador Dali, in the flesh.

   And the flesh was haggard and old, caked in futile layers
of makeup which, mixed with the deep lines there, gave
his face the look of a puppet. But his movements were still
quite spry as he led the woman toward the curb, toward
me. I had the door opened by this time, but I was fairly
mesmerized. It was easy to see why my eyes were drawn
from the woman to him. He had a magnetic presence, and
it went far beyond the oddity of his moustache (though up
close that thing was pretty fucking wild). The two of them
were perfect examples of those variations in *presence* which
I've written about before: it was the difference between a
chimpanzee and a cheetah. She was the monkey; he was
the cat.

   And the cat was now stepping off the curb, the chimp
at his side. I didn't have any idea what he wanted. I aroused
a quick fantasy of him embracing me and laying a kiss on
both cheeks and exclaiming, "Brother artist! I know your
work well, and envy it even more. The first half of the
century was mine, but clearly the second half has passed
into your hands . . . here, take the woman . . . she is yours

forever!" That's not exactly how it went down, however. Instead, they acted as if they were on some esplanade in Venice, and I was a peasant holding steady the plank to the gondola for them. He lifted up his cane to my knees and, as I'm still holding the door, he used it to softly hold me back. The woman entered the cab, giving me a look that said something along the lines of, "God, what is *that* doing here, I thought I had the valet scrape it from my boots this morning!" Dali himself was gushing, smiling at me and swinging back his cane, entering the cab as if all this were as it should be. I was awestruck. I was for some reason seeing myself at fifteen, looking at his painting "The Crucifixion" in the Met for the first time. With my mouth hanging open, the painter slammed shut the cab door, leaving me sprawling on the hood of a parked car. I raced back over to the cab, where to my amazement, Dali was opening the window and looking up at me, *"Bonjour!"* he spoke, effusive and loud, and the taxi sprang off, like a horse slapped on the rump.

I hadn't said a word . . . I might as well have had my dick in my hand, cursed, naked and supine. Imagine, popped by a surrealist! It entered my mind to yell something hideous at the cab which was stuck in traffic only three car-lengths away, something like, *Weirdo-frog creep . . . hype be thy savior . . . you wouldn't be diddly shit if it wasn't for that moustache! How'd you like it if I snipped half of it off . . . I'm nobody's fool . . . I've got scissors here, and I know how to use them!*

But I couldn't do that, not to Salvador Dali, not to the man who embraced me in such a hastily conjured fantasy, passing on the torch of Art, as it were. I just raised up my hand, with half-parted lips, and waved. *"Bonjour, Monsieur Dali,"* I muttered. *"Bonjour et adieu."*

THE DALAI LAMA

This friend of mine, a performance artist of outrageous excesses, just returned from India. He was off, on the tail end of the serpentine horde before him, to find the Light Supreme. I'd hardly have suspected him as a guru-clutcher type, but there you have it: You just never know. At any rate, there he was, sitting on a metal stoop along 8th Street as I was crossing east.

"The trip was a bust," he mumbled, adjusting the tongue of his shoe (which amazingly seemed to be creeping down through the laces on its own initiative), "I mean, dig this. I met the Dalai Lama himself . . . the *Lama*, for Christ's sake . . . the honcho of single syllable secrets . . . the top fucking banana . . ."

"I've heard of him, yeah, he's big . . ." I interjected hesitantly.

"*Big*? . . . shit, he is the *Man* . . . I mean he . . ."

"I saw Tarzan save him, or a *roman à clef*, non-litigious facsimile, last Sunday morning!" I cut in.

"You know what he wanted from me?" he went on, a warning in his eye and tone not to cut in again. "What he wanted, after this forty-five minutes of my well-tuned peroration *cum* biography and questions, was to see me do some fucking card tricks . . . can you imagine? Card tricks!"

"You mentioned in your bio-rap your background in magic, huh?" I shot in very quickly, moving down a step's distance from him.

"Sure, naturally. Prestidigitation, sleight of hand . . . I had made mention of that, sure. But the questions I had asked were of enormous . . ."

"Did you have a deck of cards?"

"What?"

"A deck of cards, did you have one?" I moved down another step . . . I was one away from squatting on the pavement.

"No, I didn't," he answered, not really angry I mentioned it. In fact, he seemed to switch gears. "That was the thing, too—no cards, even my Tarot deck was ruined when some crazy Dutch kid tossed my shoulderbag in the Ganges as I was bathing. I did, however, have the canned lobster bisque trick with me."

"The *what* trick?" I asked, shuttling back up a step.

"You know, I did it at one of the Monday-night readings at St. Mark's when you were working there running the thing . . . I take a can of lobster bisque and put a hand-kerchief over it, make a hand pass or two and open the can with your regular run-of-the-mill opener and pour it out and it turns out to be one single blob of . . ."

"Cranberry sauce!" I half-leapt up, yelling loud enough for a passing tourist-type to turn his head at us and careen off a parking meter.

"Right!" he was pleased, "And the Lama really . . ."

"It was ravioli," I muttered. Another step down.

"Ravioli, what? I was telling you that the Lama . . ."

"At St. Mark's you transformed a can of ravioli not lobster bisque!"

"Okay," he pressed on, "It was ravioli, for God's sake . . . I used bisque for the Dalai Lama. The point is that he was amazed by it. He clapped his sacred hands for two minutes and guffawed."

"The Dalai Lama guffawed?" I said. "And he didn't figure out that it was simply a matter of you having switched a lobster bisque label onto the cranberry sauce can before-hand?"

"AHA!" He made eye contact for the first time. I could see from that washed out look that he was a real satori vigilante . . . "If you'll recall, *you* didn't figure it out either at St. Mark's. I remember you bugging me for the secret."

"That's true, I remember, that's true," I concurred, "but the Lama really dug it, eh? Guffawed? That's great, and it makes me feel good to know that the Dalai Lama himself was as fooled by the same simple trick as I."

"Well," he spoke, standing up and beginning to walk,

"the fact is, he did figure it out . . . though not for a minute
or two. What really got him was the initial shock. The
textural switch, you see; he never felt a solid blob of cranberry sauce before. It was some tactile fetish. He loved the
feel of it so much that he palmed the fucking blob and
gave it to an aide to keep."

ROCK 'N' ROLL

I have been considering lately writing lyrics for some rock-
and-roll bands. Certain friends have prompted me toward
this idea for years. Some, like Jenny Ann, have even made
the ridiculous proposition that I *sing* these songs . . . that
I actually front a band! They tell me they see the possibilities when I give readings of my poems and diaries. The
way I move. The phrasing.

I do believe that a poet would possess a stronger intuitive
sense of phrasing with a rock song . . . that there is a way
to tap into the emotions of an audience simply by the cross
of a certain phrase, even a single word, against a certain
chord. There's no doubt in my mind. But I respect craft.
I believe in technique . . . and my singing abilities are so
serious a handicap that it would take a whole new scale to
make the entire thing less than ludicrous. Music without
melody, where my voice would simply be another rhythm
instrument, like a drum.

But why even go on considering such matters (and I see
myself trying here, as I move from sentence to sentence,
to talk, or rather write, myself into the possibility)? The
fact is that I am horrified to face a modest-sized audience
at readings, when I understand (and trust) my capabilities.
I shudder, literally feel a spread-open hand guiding up my
intestine, a spiked armadillo in my belly, at the thought of
facing a rock audience under the weight of my mistrust
and limitations. But do I need to prove to anyone at this
point that I am a fool, and that I seem to enjoy hauling
around the weights of excess on my shoulders, in my guts,

in my brittle mind? I have yet to destroy my reflexes, however, built strong by athletics and poetry. It would be better if I did. They are a vice rather than a gift. I am too quick; I have used this quickness to destroy myself. I use it to steal things from my own pockets, my own hands, my own inclinations.

Yet, I would like to see fame to understand it. I would like to hold it in my hands a while, like a crawling infant with a ball of yarn . . . to unravel it and realize what I believe I already know, that the core is empty. Then I could dismiss it and crawl away. But I expect it would not be that easy . . . getting far enough away once you are on your knees.

LOST ON THE BACK OF MY HAND

For the most part since my return to New York City, I have avoided the parties and art scene events, preferring to ride shotgun on my rehabilitation regimen from my apartment in the wilds of upper, upper Manhattan. I thought I would return to the fast social life of New York, but I've continued my reclusive period here, content, confused, studious and somewhat sublime. In particular, I have avoided like a leaky reactor my old haunts such as Max's Kansas City. It's one thing to sneak about and try to cold-cock fate from behind, but it is another thing altogether to walk straight up and spit in its face. There are too many white-powdered memories which I've left spilled on the floors of those places, too many faces with too little in their eyes.

But the peculiar, inbred species of *chance* which thrives in this city can tap you any moment, anywhere, its sticky fingers either caressing your neck or inserting themselves directly into your eye. It approached me this evening with a combination of both techniques. I was in the subway, home of the most virulent strains of chance.

I was going home after an afternoon of movies, about

to descend the stairs to the uptown "A" train platform at 59th and Columbus Circle. I heard a female voice directed at me, but calling out the name "Rolf." I turned anyway. It was a tall blonde, maybe thirty years old, though it was hard to tell. Her hair was cut short, her eyes stunning and strange, like those of a doll made in the shop-class of a school for disturbed young girls. Even their color was unsettling. They were the strangulated blue of a cardiac victim's fingers. They were strained and defeated, with the promiscuity of one who has let go of a failure only they themselves perceive. It was hard to tell how she was built; her clothes were baggy and dark. The buttons to the blouse beneath her open coat, however, were undone far enough to reveal the wide cleavage of large, braless breasts. Overall, she was beautiful, and the closer she approached the more beautiful she became.

"Rolf, don't you pretend with me," she spoke in a thick German accent, "that you do not recognize your own sister!"

"I'm afraid you are mistaken . . ." I began.

"Do not play with me now, not now." She reached out and touched my cheek. I pulled back.

"I'm not your brother, really," I insisted in a louder voice, trying not to put her off completely because, to tell you the truth, I was still carrying around that exorbitant horniness that inevitably follows withdrawal.

"Very well, play this foolish game," she also seemed miffed, "but come with me now to my friend's party."

I hesitated a moment. This could turn out to be a disaster, I told myself. Then again, I *was* back in New York, and I did long for a little of the old adventure, to play out an anonymous night like the old days, to let down the shields of control I had constructed, just for a while. It had been so long since my instincts were ruled by my body, specifically my cock, that I figured they deserved a chance to be given the lead. I took the stranger's hand from my cheek, where it was continuing to caress and call me "brother," and led her out of the subway and onto the street. I asked her where the party was, telling her we should take a cab. She reached in her purse for a slip of paper with the address as I flagged a big Checker. We got in and she read off the address to the driver, who looked at her severely upon hearing her accent. From his age I could tell he was a vet of World War II, and the German intonation brought back the memory of flies in tins of food, and the corpses of dead buddies.

"Do you know where it is?" I asked, to cool him out, assuring him that this kraut bitch was in the hands of a real American. He looked at me like I was even worse scum, however.

"I know where it is," he said, his grip strangling the wheel.

It was good he did know the address because, though I pride myself on knowing Manhattan like the back of my hand, this street sounded unfamiliar. All the streets were empty of people, gone home from work hours before. The buildings were either tall office spaces or industrial lofts. I realized that I really didn't know this area at all. I might as well have been in Cleveland. I had been staring at the woman so intently in the cab while she went on and on about "our" parents, the cruel father and sweet but hapless mother, that I hadn't followed the cab's route and had no points of reference to fix on, except when the cabbie mumbled some obscene reference to the mayor as we passed City Hall. I was lost in Manhattan, and that was a very unpleasant sensation. I had smoked a joint of some wicked grass for the movie I went to. It was the one drug indulgence I still allowed myself, knowing that if God didn't want us to smoke grass, he wouldn't have put movie theaters on His green earth. Now the grass was turning on me, spurred on by this sense of being stranded in unexplored territory in *my own city*. We found the address, though. It was an industrial building, a bit shabby on the outside. We pressed a buzzer next to a mailbox and two doors parted

of their own electronic initiative. We stood in the hall, waiting for an elevator. There were about six other people
waiting there as well. If they were going to the same party,
they were either seriously overdressed or my "sister" and
I were terrifyingly underdressed. My "sister," whose name
I finally learned as she described a scene of her father
beating her while yelling her name repeatedly, was Sigrid;
she told me that the girl giving the party was an old, old
friend of hers, an actress who went to Hollywood from
Hamburg with Sigrid in the mid-sixties. Sigrid was an actress as well. While working in England, she told me, she
had done a bunch of those Daughter of Frankenstein/Bride
of Dracula pictures. In the cab, she also showed me a four-
page layout of herself in some porno magazine. She obviously, and somewhat pathetically, carried it folded up in
her purse. It had, by the worn creases, clearly been folded
and unfolded countless times to show anyone who cared
to look. She was thinner in the pictures, which were, by
the magazine's date, over five years old, and in them her
hair was very long and lustrous. At first I thought it wasn't
really her, but as the taxi passed down a more brightly lit
street, I could see that, despite more wear on her than five
years should be permitted to inflict, the girl in the pictures
and the woman beside me, insisting I was her brother, were
the same.

We stood there waiting for the elevator, and she smiled
at me and held her arms to my waist. Even the way she
held me was more like the affectionate, playful embrace
of a sister for her brother than anything else. I liked her
smile in the fluorescent brightness of that hall. I liked her.
I couldn't imagine (or couldn't allow myself to imagine)
that she really thought I was her brother. It was all a pretense leading up to some incest-oriented sexual game. Of
course I knew she was crazed, but I was not going to consider how deep it went, or how far it might go. I didn't
sense any danger, and, being high on grass and ripe for
paranoia, I was certain of my instincts as far as *that* went.

I smiled back at her and, for the first time, grabbed her and kissed her, brotherly at first, then far beyond that. She reciprocated. The elevator arrived and its doors opened. It was huge inside, with deep, posh carpeting. One of the others pushed the fifth-floor button. Sigrid didn't move, so I knew we were, indeed, all going to the same place, same party. She didn't seem upset about the incongruity of our dress compared with the others, who had put as much space between us as the large elevator allowed. There were two men and four women. The men were in formal evening wear, the women in gowns. Although all were attractive, one woman in particular caught my eye.

She was mesmerizingly beautiful, in a black velvet dress and diamond earrings and necklace. It was certain she was a model. She had the look, and she had the essential slump of the body and tilt of the head.

It was the kind of beauty which, if I saw her in a hotel lobby, would make me dash to my room until I could catch my breath and cease trembling. She had the looks that send me so deep into longing that there is physical pain. It is a pain which begins in the ears, a scream from some damp, anguished muse. The pressure then turns inward, heads to the heart like a wind too thick for its passage through my veins, so it creates a path of its own. You find yourself in the corner of the room you ran to, almost choking.

And what is it you want? It is not sexual, though you do want her. You want her because, in some unfathomed way, she is the *proof*, the proof of those things you always knew existed but could not define. Yet you've had women like this in the past, and in the end they proved nothing. They solved nothing. They were usually not too bright and were terribly self-indulgent. They were, as this one is, only another emblem of your own vanity, and the vanity of your Art.

I understand all this, looking at her now, as she avoids my stare while still giving everything away. I understand but it makes no difference. She offers me something time-

less, and I begin to fantasize right there. I imagine her
pubic hair clipped in the shape of some lost continent, its
edges littered with shells and pink and blue anemones.
There is the salt-sharp smell of a civilization there, ruined
by heat and flood at its glory, many times over, yet destined,
always, to rise again.

Sigrid breaks my take as she asks none of them in particular if they know Danielle, her friend giving the party.
Nobody answers, they just turn to face the elevator, knowing it is about to stop at our floor. And it does. They exit,
then Sigrid, who I am actually beginning to feel protective
of, and I do the same.

The moment we step into the place, something clicks
wrong in me. For one thing, Sigrid's "friend" Danielle is
about as happy to see her as some Venusian plague. She
looks at Sigrid in unmasked disgust, barely offering any
greeting. When Sigrid asks her if there is a spare room
that she can use, Danielle makes a vague gesture with her
finger, then hurries to speak to someone else.

It's clear Sigrid wants to take her little brother into the
spare room to screw, but first she asks if we should get a
drink. I say okay, and we proceed to a fancy bar. It's a
strange scene. The space, despite the building's ratty facade, is vast and sumptuous. It's like one huge loft space
with networks of side rooms. There are mammoth sculp-
tures everywhere, some rising upward from the floor, others hanging from the ceiling. There is a labyrinthine
configuration of metal gongs which guests pass through in
the middle of the main room, so chiming is heard, faintly
but continuously, over the stereo as bodies brush against
them. The furniture is sleek, cold and modern.

The people are all dressed as fine as our fellow passengers in the elevator. They stink of bitter, inherited wealth.
There are accents from every nook and cranny of the European continent represented, merging in a Babel-esque
cacophony. Cocaine is being passed around openly on glass

trays. I've heard about the proliferation of this drug, of its conquest as drug of choice by the smart Eurotrash quasi-aristocratic set, but this is something to behold. I notice the stunning girl from the elevator packing a line up her nose. She looks at me with a gleeful disdain. Some warm, unpleasant sensation comes over me. I pity her for the despair that must, I am certain, lie beneath her aloofness, yet, at the same time, I pity myself for the aloofness in my own despair.

I saw right then that anything went at that address, but nothing could have prepared me for the scene that I, almost literally, stumbled upon. Walking quickly, with Sigrid holding my hand like some killer vine, I caught my foot on a plank of wood, almost falling head-first. It turned out to be the border of a sandbox, right there in the room, and in the sandbox were two naked guys going strong on one naked woman, front and back. I couldn't believe it. An erudite older man, impeccably dressed and sporting a walking stick, stood next to me, obviously both amused and aroused by the event. He told me it was his wife, and taking notice of me because of my played-down attire of jeans and leather jacket, asked me if I "wanted to have a go at her." He had a snide little smile, and a voice that matched. His teeth were yellow like the eyes of a sheep. His eyes were like children's blocks . . . the ones that have letters on the face of each side. His skin was pock-marked, an emblem of the vanity and impatience of his youth. I had never seen a man with such total confidence in his own perversity.

I ducked under a tray and moved off. The sounds trailed up from the fuck-filled sandbox like dogs whining from a nightmare. I wanted to reach that room with Sigrid. I looked at the faces. It was like moving through a jungle. The faster you moved, the more you were consumed by their decay, body and soul. The harder you struggled to reach some exit from those eyes, the faster the process spread, until eventually you were devoured. Their every movement was a cluster of pretense and artifice. Their energy to squander was limitless. Into this energy they tossed everything they lacked, having long ago wasted everything they had.

These are the people who never raised a mitt to the sky, who never felt a ball spin from their fingertips toward a broken hoop in a schoolyard, who never dropped a coin in the extended can of a fake charity along Fifth Avenue at midday. These were the people who never shielded their eyes with their hands to see a ring that moved around the sun.

I found the room Danielle had shown Sigrid and threw open the door. A couple injecting themselves with coke, I presume, in their leg veins, scurried off like kitchen roaches in the three A.M. light of a refrigerator door. Sigrid was acting strange. It had not escaped my attention that she was scarfing coke from every tray that passed. I looked at her on the bed, but the smile had changed. It had that dangerous look of schizophrenic lust. She lay back and began a monologue on being back in our home in Germany as children. Our father's motorcycle could be heard approaching in the distance, and she was scared. He was going to be filthy and intolerant from the drinking after work. He would beat her. She began crying. She was crying in the house where she grew up, and she was crying on the bed where she lay now, with me looking down on her.

Then she grabbed something small and, I assume, valuable beside the bed and threw it at the wall. As it smashed, she raised her eyes to me with a spider-like desire, her eyes moist with anger or passion or regret. I moved backward calmly, and opened the door. I told her I had to piss. I told her I would be right back.

The fact was, I did have to piss, and badly, but I had no intention of returning. She was too much, and getting worse by the minute. As I shut the door I could see her hand down her pants playing with herself. She called out her brother's name breathlessly as she came to orgasm with remarkable speed. I stood there, hearing her moaning and evoking "Rolf," with the door half-closed behind me, not wanting to advance into that licentious jungle outside, yet equally hesitant to retreat back into her line of schizoid fire and lust. Between a fucking rock and a hard place, to be sure.

I wondered why I didn't just go in and jump her bones. She was remarkable sexy, and the sister-brother incest scenario was right out of the catalogue of my jerk-off fantasies, filed right up on the top shelf, in fact. These people might disgust me in myriad ways, but that never stopped me before. If anything, it was an enhancement.

It wasn't the same with this fräulein, however. I knew the hazards of schizophrenic sexmates. With each fuck they invent a new persona, reaching deeper and deeper into darker recesses of the lunatic pools. Eventually, one of the personas she dredges up and instills in herself is out of control, and dangerously so. That was the difference in me now: I valued control these days as strongly as I totally disregarded it before. I realized that too much of what she had could get inside my head and nest, could incubate there and, in time, hatch. I was sick of giving evil and misery an edge in my life, of always offering them the advantage of the first move. I knew from experience that after we had fuck-finished, her body would go limp, so limp her skin would sag like a cheap, overused stocking across the sheets. All those personas she borrowed from madness and orgasm would be gone, leaving that moment of complete evanescence. The shell of her body would be left sprawled across the bed, and confused tears would flow until she was lucky enough to sleep.

So I shut the door behind me, still hearing the sounds of her masturbation. It was so strange: dual sounds, like the growl of a rabid animal dubbed over a child's sighs. It was coming from two separate places, two separate persons. I could swear to that.

I moved through the crowd to find a bathroom. I could feel easier about checking out this horrid slime now that I

was safe in the thought that I'd soon be gone. It was fascinating, and the grass, which I was still feeling buzzed
from, brought more and more out front. For example, I
noticed the shadows of people standing over against the
wall next to the sandbox, where the same woman was getting bi-banged, urged on by her pock-marked husband,
who was now being openly sucked off by a naked boy,
blond, beautiful and no older than fifteen. These shadows,
the shadows of people who have lost their nerve as well as
their feeling, seemed weaker against the wall than other
people's. In some instances, certain fragments of these bodies gave off no shadow at all. I imagined their blood was
thinner too.

I found a bathroom up a short, well-carpeted, circular
staircase. It seemed empty when I opened the door. It was
as impressive as everything else in the place: large and
bright, the rug so thick naked feet would disappear in it.
I walked in, and as I turned to shut the door behind me,
saw I was not alone. There was a man to my right, completely naked, his formal wear folded on the rug beside
him in a neat pile. He was standing there with a modest
hard-on, jerking off. It was so modest in its size that, even
though it was quite erect, the most he could get around it
was two fingers and his thumb. He jiggled it furiously with
this digital triad. His eyes were fixed, almost in a trance,
staring into the mirrors cornering the bathtub. The image
of the man repeated itself over and over, like the picture
of the man on a Quaker Oats box. You know what I mean.
The image grows smaller each time, but extends in theory
on to infinity. So, in that sense, he was standing there jerking off with an endless row of selves, each with the same
lascivious glint in the eyes, each with the same salacious
tongue flicking through the same grotesque smile, with lips
thin as salmon fillets smashed over and over by a wooden
mallet. It was the ultimate act of narcissism, and I couldn't
deny to myself that it was a pretty sexy operation—if, that
is, it wasn't being performed right in my face by such a

short-hung weasel. He turned his head slightly as I appeared in the mirror, shattering his trance. Without stopping, he asked me not to get in his reflected view, or it would spoil the whole effect.

"Isn't it *the end*?" he spoke in a voice sounding like he had just sucked a helium balloon dry. "I'm doing it with an endless row of my own body! What could be sexier?"

"A better body," I muttered, "for openers."

"Except, of course . . ." and he hesitated, "if *you* might want to join in. We could do each other."

"No thanks, really."

"But, and be honest now, couldn't you just *die*?"

"Yes," I added flatly, washing my hands, "As a matter of fact, I could."

He went back into his trance, his tongue lashing furiously from his face. I dried off my hands on my jeans, not wanting to catch anything that was possibly aristocratic from the towels. I opened the door and spoke: "Just remember, if you really look hard enough, if you really look far enough, you'll see, in the end, just how very small you are. In fact, you'll see that, eventually, you just fade away, disappear."

I shut the door and went down the staircase. I was sick, tired, stoned and weirded out, and I was angry as well. I put out my arms and slashed aside the crowd like branches and thick foliage. That's how you move through a jungle. Even the lush carpet felt like quicksand beneath my feet. I moved faster. By the time I reached the elevator, I had actually knocked one clown on his ass. Fortunately the elevator was right there as I pushed the button. I descended in its large confines, this time all alone.

When I reached the street I was in a sweat, glad to be free of that scum-tide but realizing I was lost. I took in a deep breath of good New York air, unpolluted by French scents. It made me feel better. I was loose and clear, even if I was out of bounds. I began walking.

Up the block, I looked down a dim-lit alley and saw two huge dogs climbing with grace and ease out the window of a stripped-down Ford, its axles raised on cinderblocks. "That looks like a better party than the one I came from," I yelled at the canines, who were illuminated by the dim light of an office above. The dogs stared back, one puzzled and benign, the other with that slow growl that says, "Please move on or I will chew off a limb." I moved on, slowly at first, then breaking into a run. I was giddy to be lost, glad to be anywhere outside that luxurious hole I left, but I wanted to get home. I ran faster. The streets were totally abandoned, not one person in sight. Then, to my majestic surprise, a lone Checker cab turned a corner, very slowly, one block up and headed my way, moving as if it were searching all this time for me, as if it had been sent.

OPENING NIGHT

After that fiasco of a party last night, all I want to do is lose it. I woke up late, after one of those frustrating sleeps that is like trying to write when nothing's coming. I figure the only way to shake last night's deep downer is hard drugs or the movies. I opt for the latter, not out of any great nobility of will, but simply because I don't have the same energy and cunning as I used to when it comes to bull-shitting myself these days. These days . . . God, they seem so fucking *full* when you're clean. I go out to find a paper. See what's playing.

I decide on a triple feature of Hitchcock down on Broadway at the Thalia. One of them, *Rope*, I've actually not seen before. The other two, *Strangers on a Train* and *Suspicion*, are . . . well, they're Hitchcock. There's no more to be said.

Afterwards, I exit with that strange exhilaration of post-Hitchcockian intensity. I visit a poet friend of mine who lives nearby. We smoke some more and listen to some tunes. I realize I'm totally out of it as far as what's happening these days on the music scene. I haven't heard of any of these new bands.

"You must have been living in a cave on the West Coast," he jokes.

"You're not too far off," I answer. "And if I hear much more of this shit music, I might get back, fast . . . and the next cave will be much deeper."

He seems visibly insulted. That's the way it is with these dudes who pride themselves on their voluminous record collections. Then they take your dislike for some band from Detroit personally. My friend Lenny's the one exception, and he's got everything ever croaked onto vinyl or tape. Otherwise, you don't like a record and guys like my friend here tonight act as if you just stuck a razor blade into a piece of liverwurst and fed it to their dog. That's okay, I'd feel the same way if he played these records to my dog. I split, treating myself to a cab uptown.

So I get home and, as if I hadn't had enough cinema for the day, turn on the late show. It is *Paths of Glory* by Kubrick, perhaps my all-time favorite movie, excluding all the others. I move the TV into the bathroom and place it on the toilet seat, plug it into the socket next to the sink which, I suppose, is used for electric razors. I run the water to take a hot bath, watch the movie within the pleasures of steam, and evaporate perhaps the demons that have embedded themselves into my muscles. I get naked and enter the red tub. Yes, that's right, I live in an apartment with a red bathtub. The previous tenant must have done it. Not only is it red, but the paint job is crude, with thick textural squiggles which abuse your skin from any and all positions. At first I thought it was a good conversation piece, but then I realized there was rarely anyone else here to converse with, aside from a few women now and then who did not seem to notice it or made comments like, "Your tub's red." Now it just makes me feel like I'm washing in a kosher abattoir, or, worse still, I get up to piss half-asleep some nights, and turn on the light to sudden accusations in my still supine consciousness that I am some brutal slasher who hacked his victim here, disposed of the body, but forgot to clean up on returning, and instead, gave in to exhaustion and just fell out on the bed. I have to check my hands for signs of blood and organs.

I'm relaxing in the bath, the water very hot and only one rather soft dollop of red paint pressed against my ass. It's just the scene in the movie where Ralph Meeker, playing one of the French soldiers about to be executed within hours on trumped-up charges of cowardice, makes the rather orotund remark as he watches a cockroach seize a crumb on the table, "Tomorrow that roach will still exist . . . it will still be alive, and I shall be nothing." Then, in response to this, Timothy Carey, with wild eyes and sarcastic lips lunging at the camera, plays out one of the all-time highlights of the cinema. He slowly raises his hand and "Whack!" The bug is crushed, squashed, no longer alive, non-existent. He turns to Meeker and mutters soberly, "There, you feel better now?"

It never fails to grab me. I laugh so hard the water rocks to and fro, as if it too got the joke, and spills out vastly onto the floor, where it divides and slides down into the crevices of cracked tile. I can almost hear the screams of silverfish rudely awakened. They slither out of their lodgings and disappear just as quickly under the sink. I admire the alternatives insects have in the way of housing. They're the only ones getting over in New York City.

The movie ends. A priest comes on the air and conveys a rather tick-in-the-eye-like platitude. I am out of action by the water's heat. I want to get up, but my brain is steamed to mush and ether, and I can't hack the idea of standing up into the vicious chill of this apartment. I decide to turn the tap back on to fortify the heat and wait it out until the radiator starts steaming, thus equalizing the ratio of water-room temperatures.

Since I have no book, I'm stranded with my own thoughts. The TV channel has just signed off after the National Anthem played with a backdrop of Titan missiles launched

and flooding the sky. You need a color TV to fully appreciate such images, I suppose. Now there's just a test pattern
and an annoying tone of high frequency. I turn the sound
down. What if I were to knock the TV into the water as I
were turning the knob? I wonder if the effect of the shock
would be agony or pleasure, or if at that point one could
tell the difference? For that matter, I wonder if the moment
of death itself would be . . . *no, no way* . . . I don't care if
the TV's bare. I'm not getting into *that shit*. Not in a red
bathtub. Not with the water so hot. "Lobster" metaphysics.
I'm just glad I walked away from that slime at that dreary
party last night. No matter how fine the women, or how
hard they came on. I think I did learn some things in
California. I believe I have moved closer to my heart. I feel
comfortable in reclusion. I don't need the vacant flux of
parties. I don't need my own attendance at "Art Happenings" which are, for the most part, excuses for the party
afterward. But I don't want to become a cynical prick. It
is, after all, a human universe. Knowledge, the hunger for
detail, even the learned trivia, *does* give way to wisdom. If
you don't push. If you sit back and remove the clutter of
lips and claws and capsules and punch. I *know* I *am* a cold
motherfucker, but I *have* moved closer to my heart.

Strange how long it takes to write out notions that pass
by in seconds while laid out in a red bathtub, waiting for
the first sounds of the heat rising in the radiator. I'm halfway to sleep now. Though my painter friend D.M.Z. does
it all the time, I only fell asleep once in a bathtub. That
was a long time ago. I shut my eyes and words pass over
the lids, which feel like they have been scraped
clean . . . hollowed out. And stuffed with words. A long
time ago . . . when I slept in a tub. That was when I thought
an oxymoron was a beautiful flower. White with blue bands,
most likely. With those thin stems with globes on the end,
like honeysuckle, growing from the center. A tournament
for winged insects.

Words passing upright, like troops for inspection. "*Ichor.*"

"*Uxorious*." "*Thump*." "*Ichneumon*." "*Vatorphobia*": the fear of starving to death in a stalled elevator.

I hear the wasp-like hiss of the radiators. They have woken me from my sleep, from dreaming of words, and later of women in 1920s hairdos and modern lingerie. Two hours have passed, and my body is the color and texture of a cauliflower. When I first woke I panicked, seeing the red globs on the tub's bottom. I thought I was trapped with a hideous wound, in the engine room of some sinking luxury liner, just treading above a decreasing waterline. I snapped out fast, however. The elapsed time had lowered the water to a sobering temperature, and I was out quickly, toweling off beside the thick pipe, emitting heat from floor to ceiling. I put on my robe and carried the TV into the bedroom, placing it on its usual crate.

I could have fallen asleep immediately, but I read a bit. Watch the TV without sound. The Roadrunner is zipping through deserts, leaving the Coyote reading a manual in thick clouds of dust. The silence is eerie; it always is at this time of night in New York City. All that time spent in the country out in California, sleeping to the orchestrations of strange tiny things making strange loud noises, has given me an awareness of this New York City silence which makes it staggering and, at times, plain fearsome. After all, I grew up with this silence. I'm not talking about the sounds of the Village or forty-deuce here. Those places are non-stop; might as well be Vegas. I'm talking about the New York *neighborhoods*, the areas where the people live on the time of working stiffs. This silence is almost visual. You expect shadowless things to dart out. You anticipate the most horrific scenes . . . with the quick fall of high heels on subway gratings, your spine pulls up like a horse rearing. And you're *always* expecting *the scream* to come, of women or air-raid sirens.

Then there is the sound of sweet continuity . . . the perorations of morning. The bakery trucks with twenty-year-old transmissions, their gears changing loud as a construction site at noon in midtown. The news truck at 5:30 A.M., where the guy yells out and the bales of *The New York Times* hit the pavement with a stiffer thump than the *News* or the *Post*. An old guy who wears the same red-and-black flannel jacket and cap in the heat of summer and the freeze of winter mutters something back through toothless gums, then rises off his milk crate and slices the stacks of information open, like hay, with a wicked razor-knife. A few faithful dog-walkers hand him change (I can hear the change), then separate their tangled leashes and split. And the garbage trucks . . . I almost forgot. They come earlier, maybe four A.M. They break the silence with otherworldly noises. When I was a kid, I always thought when their sound sometimes woke me, that there were aliens on Broadway disposing of humans who had found them out, like meat through a grinder. The sound made me press my teeth together and grind so hard my jaw would ache all day through school. But the Department of Sanitation has already come and gone for tonight.

I put down my book. It's 4:45. I pull the plug on the TV. The flashing ghosts on the screen condense deep into themselves, then blackness. I'm about to turn off the light when I notice the green slime leaking down by forearm. The indestructible abscess in the pit of my elbow, which should be celebrating its second birthday anytime now, is really overflowing tonight. It's no wonder, now that I think about it: all that time submerged in the bath, the hot water loosening up all that awful crud. It's drooling from the same tiny opening at its bottom. I grab a tissue, spit on it, and wipe my forearm clean. Normally, when it leaks so profusely, I am tempted to have a go at the thing . . . to squeeze the feisty source from all angles, hoping it will finally burst totally, and set its healing in motion. But I'm too wiped out for the challenge, which is exactly what this thing has become. It tempts me with a drop of ooze, then for hours I'm in a free-for-all with my gross nemesis, pinching and piercing from right and left, up and down. It always wins. I extract a bit of vile fluid, but the source remains intact. The fucking doctors tell me it's not worth lancing, that it will heal itself. They don't have to deal with its spite, its enticements to self-mutilation, the exhaustion of its resistance: body, mind and soul. It's taken on demonic proportions. Shit, I've *sanctified* the motherfucker: I caress it in my sleep.

I'm just going to accept it. I'm tired.

I reach again for the light. But I hesitate. Maybe just one little tweak. I mean that fucker was really flowing. I've wiped it twice and there's still slime reappearing.

All right then, but just one shot at it. Just a survey of the situation. I'm too tired; getting beaten down would only wake me up. I extend my right arm, which contains the beastly little apparatus. I take my left hand and, with thumb and forefinger on opposite sides of the wound, seek out the proper dimensions to attack. This is the point when, no matter how often I've failed, my hopes are revivified. My stomach tightens. I think about my cat choking from an abscess back in California, and the wonderful feeling I had of opening that wound, watching the scum pour out, and the lovely sound of the creature breathing anew, sucking in the air of *another chance*. I want that sensation. No matter how much I've cleaned up, this hole in my arm is still an emblem of my addiction, a memorial tattoo that I myself inscribed, as if for an old lover, in homage to that sickness I took years to perfect.

My fingers are in place, a little farther apart than usual. A strange feeling creeps over me, like when I was a ballplayer and I somehow *knew* I couldn't miss. I pinch the two fingers together, slow and steady, that strange sensation guiding me to apply just the right pressure, as it did with my fingertips years ago when I aimlessly released a basketball at the hoop. The funky slime is rapidly escaping . . . it feels looser beneath the skin than before, from all that time in the hot water as I slept in the tub. But still there is no final burst.

I increase the pressure, changing the angle of my thumb. I press tighter . . . green gunk seeps out, dripping from my arm . . . the feeling has my head reeling . . . I can't *miss* . . . tighter now . . . oh, my God . . . *it explodes.*

Out it flows, not just from that small opening, but from the center, in one stream, like a laser's beam. It exits in various shades of yellow and green, followed by blood. When that stubborn skin finally gave way, after all that time, I thought I heard an audible expression, like a groan, or a tired, breathless howl of someone who lost a long, long duel. I could swear it. I could swear I heard that sound.

I grabbed some cotton balls and peroxide from the drawer of the night table beside the bed, remembering all the nights I applied it in frustration. But I didn't swab it yet, I kept on pressing. I wanted the last vestiges of that horror within. I wanted to prolong the feeling of victory. There was no feeling of disgust for the slime, or the pools it had formed on my sheets. All disgust was overwhelmed by joy. Besides, you must understand: this was not just some infected body fluids I was looking down on. To me, this was the return of all the bad-cut street-drug garbage I had inserted with such precision, all these years. This was the toxic residue of all my past sins (there, I've said it!). I didn't see pus; I saw the petty demons marching out. I saw purification, with *new fresh air* being sucked into that cavity, like the cat. The idol was in ruins. Do you understand what I'm telling you? I know you think it's sick, some fucked-up fetish. No doubt. But I understand the nature of it, and now that sickness is healing. So am I. I might very well blow it again. I don't really know where I go from here, but at least I've raised my quality of living above cockroach level. New York is not the same, that's for certain. I feel, as I said, closer to my heart. I feel a comfort in being alone. *And, momma, I don't want to make the scene no more.*

But I'm not worrying about all that right now. I want to penetrate only this moment. I've pierced a veil. I've beaten an old enemy and I'm tired and my mind is clear, my senses full. I can hear that bakery truck just pulling away down on Broadway, leaving behind only the stunned silence of New York City at 5:15 A.M. It's so quiet I can hear the clicking of the traffic lights changing . . . red to green . . . stop to go. Walk. Wait.